GBHS
W9-ATY-461
22.96

The Discovery of the AIDS Virus

Other books in the At Issue in History series:

The Attack on Pearl Harbor
The Battle of Gettysburg
The Bill of Rights
The Conquest of the New World
The Crash of 1929
The Cuban Missile Crisis
Custer's Last Stand
The Indian Reservation System
Japanese American Internment Camps
The McCarthy Hearings
The Nuremberg Trials
Reconstruction
The Salem Witch Trials
The Sinking of the Titanic
The Tiananmen Square Massacre
The Treaty of Versailles

The Discovery of the AIDS Virus

Lisa Yount, *Book Editor*

AT ISSUE IN HISTORY

San Diego • Detroit • New York • San Francisco • Cleveland
New Haven, Conn. • Waterville, Maine • London • Munich

THOMSON
GALE

For more information, contact
Greenhaven Press
27500 Drake Rd.
Farmington Hills, MI 48331-3535
Or you can visit our Internet site at http://www.gale.com

LIBRARY OF CONGRESS CATALOGING-IN-PUBLICATION DATA

The discovery of the AIDS virus / Lisa Yount, book editor.
p. cm. — (At issue in history)
Includes bibliographical references and index.
ISBN 0-7377-1353-4 (pbk. : alk. paper) — ISBN 0-7377-1352-6 (lib. : alk. paper)
1. AIDS (Disease)—History. I. Yount, Lisa. II. Series.
RA643.8 .D575 2003
616.97'92'009—dc21 2002029814

Printed in the United States of America

Contents

Foreword

Historian Robert Weiss defines history simply as "a record and interpretation of past events." Both elements—record and interpretation—are necessary, Weiss argues.

> Names, dates, places, and events are the essence of history. But historical writing is not a compendium of facts. It consists of facts placed in a sequence to tell a connected story. A work of history is not merely a story, however. It also must analyze what happened and *why*—that is, it must interpret the past for the reader.

For example, the events of December 7, 1941, that led President Franklin D. Roosevelt to call it "a date which will live in infamy" are fairly well known and straightforward. A force of Japanese planes and submarines launched a torpedo and bombing attack on American military targets in Pearl Harbor, Hawaii. The surprise assault sank five battleships, disabled or sank fourteen additional ships, and left almost twenty-four hundred American soldiers and sailors dead. On the following day, the United States formally entered World War II when Congress declared war on Japan.

These facts and consequences were almost immediately communicated to the American people who heard reports about Pearl Harbor and President Roosevelt's response on the radio. All realized that this was an important and pivotal event in American and world history. Yet the news from Pearl Harbor raised many unanswered questions. Why did Japan decide to launch such an offensive? Why were the attackers so successful in catching America by surprise? What did the attack reveal about the two nations, their people, and their leadership? What were its causes, and what were its effects? Political leaders, academic historians, and students look to learn the basic facts of historical events and to read the intepretations of these events by many different sources, both primary and secondary, in order to develop a more complete picture of the event in a historical context.

In the case of Pearl Harbor, several important questions surrounding the event remain in dispute, most notably the role of President Roosevelt. Some historians have blamed his policies for deliberately provoking Japan to attack in order to propel America into World War II; a few have gone so far as to accuse him of knowing of the impending attack but not informing others. Other historians, examining the same event, have exonerated the president of such charges, arguing that the historical evidence does not support such a theory.

The Greenhaven At Issue in History series recognizes that many important historical events have been interpreted differently and in some cases remain shrouded in controversy. Each volume features a collection of articles that focus on a topic that has sparked controversy among eyewitnesses, contemporary observers, and historians. An introductory essay sets the stage for each topic by presenting background and context. Several chapters then examine different facets of the subject at hand with readings chosen for their diversity of opinion. Each selection is preceded by a summary of the author's main points and conclusions. A bibliography is included for those students interested in pursuing further research. An annotated table of contents and thorough index help readers to quickly locate material of interest. Taken together, the contents of each of the volumes in the Greenhaven At Issue in History series will help students become more discriminating and thoughtful readers of history.

Introduction

It started small. In New York, San Francisco, and Los Angeles in 1979 and 1980, a few physicians noticed that several of their patients had come down with—and sometimes died from—ailments so rare in the United States that they were almost unknown outside of obscure medical textbooks. Some suffered from pneumonia caused by a microscopic parasite, *Pneumocystis carinii*. Others had Kaposi's sarcoma, a slow-growing cancer-like disease that produced purple blotches on the skin and was normally found only in elderly men of Mediterranean descent. The doctors realized that these patients had features in common besides their strange illnesses: They were young, white, male, . . . and homosexual.

By 1980, these cities and a few others had sizable communities of homosexuals who made no secret of their sexuality. In San Francisco, for instance, some forty thousand gay men lived openly in a district that centered around Castro Street. They had elected a gay supervisor, Harvey Milk, to the city council in 1976. This strong showing was the result of a crusade for the right to live life their own way, free of harassment, that had begun in 1969 when a group of homosexual men at the Stonewall Inn, a gay bar in New York, had rioted against police who were raiding the club.

Young, white, well-educated, often affluent men who knew how to use the country's political system led the gay rights movement. In the 1960s–1970s era of rebellion that encompassed the drive for African American civil rights, protests against the Vietnam War, and the "free love" culture of the hippies, the gay rights movement succeeded in winning advances never before possible in the United States. However, that success was limited for the most part to these few big-city enclaves. Most Americans still saw homosexuality as a sin or a repulsive vice. In the late 1970s, conservative and religious leaders mounted backlash movements against gay rights. When Dan White, a fellow San

Francisco supervisor, assassinated Harvey Milk and liberal mayor George Moscone in 1978, he was sentenced to a mere six years in prison for the crime. Many gay men and women claimed that this light sentence reflected a belief that killing a homosexual was not important.

"This Is Going to Be Something Big"

In May 1981, even before official reports of the unusual illnesses among homosexuals appeared in medical journals, the *New York Times* heard about the New York cases and published a short article titled "Rare Cancer Seen in 41 Homosexuals." This was probably the first mention of the conditions in print. The first report in a medical publication, "*Pneumocystis* Pneumonia—Los Angeles," appeared in the *Morbidity and Mortality Weekly Report* from the Centers for Disease Control and Prevention (CDC) on June 5. Neither article attracted much attention, even among physicians, but a few scientists at the CDC and the National Institutes of Health (NIH), the group of large, government-sponsored medical research institutions in Bethesda, Maryland, began to look into the situation. One CDC researcher, Walter Dowdle, told a colleague in August, "I think this is going to be something big."

The CDC and NIH scientists came to realize that this strange collection of illnesses normally struck only people whose immune system, the body's defense system against microbes or other disease-causing agents, had been damaged. Further examination showed that in most of the patients, so-called helper or CD4 T cells, usually found in the blood and another body fluid called lymph, were almost completely missing. Without these cells, the immune system could not function. Doctors agreed that this underlying immune disorder, not the opportunistic infections it permitted, was the real problem. At first, the condition was called GRID, short for gay-related immune deficiency. No one knew what caused it or what other groups, if any, it might affect.

When reports began to surface in 1982 of similar conditions affecting users of injected drugs, who often shared hypodermic needles, and hemophiliacs, people with an inherited blood disease who had to have frequent transfusions, the scientists began to suspect that the mystery condition was infectious—caused by some kind of microorganism, probably a virus—and that it could be spread through blood as well as sex. Researchers at NIH and elsewhere studied blood and other body fluids from people with the disease, hoping to identify its cause. The same hunt was going on in Europe, where the condition had also been detected.

Rising Hysteria

While this scientific investigation was going on, awareness of the apparently new disease began to seep into the consciousness of the general public. Gay men in big cities, naturally, became aware of it first, as they saw friends and lovers die painfully and mysteriously. A group in New York founded the Gay Men's Health Crisis, the first organization to provide help for people with the disease, in late 1981.

Mainstream society initially ignored the illness, since it seemed to affect mostly groups of which most Americans disapproved. By 1983, however, the condition, now termed AIDS (acquired immune deficiency syndrome), had been found in women who had apparently been infected by having sex with infected partners and in people who had seemingly acquired the disease through blood transfusions. Al-

Cases and Deaths from AIDS in the United States, 1981–1990

Year	Cases	Deaths
1981	108	31
1982	593	243
1983	2,259	917
1984	6,993	3,342
1985	10,000	4,942
1986	28,098	15,757
1987	40,051	23,165
1988	72,024	46,134
1989	115,786	70,313
1990	161,073	100,813

Centers for Disease Control and Prevention, National Institutes of Health, AIDS Project Los Angeles.

though the disease had so far been shown to affect only about two thousand people in the United States, Americans began to feel that it could potentially strike anyone. Because the illness's cause was not known, no one could say whether it could be spread by casual contact, such as sitting next to someone with AIDS in a bus.

Instances of discrimination, not only against people with the disease but against anyone even remotely associated with it, began to multiply. Homosexuals and others in high-risk groups were fired from jobs, driven from apartments, and shunned by health care workers, acquaintances, and even sometimes members of their own families. Conservative columnist Pat Buchanan suggested barring homosexuals from all food-handling employment.

Some of the mystery surrounding AIDS ended on April 23, 1984, when Secretary of Health and Human Services Margaret Heckler announced in a widely publicized press conference that Robert Gallo, an NIH scientist, had discovered a virus that was thought to be the cause of the disease. The virus, Gallo and others said, appeared to be spread through sex and contact with infected blood, but not by casual contact. This information did little to quell anti-AIDS hysteria, however. Indeed, the hysteria increased when newspaper headlines announced in July 1985 that popular movie star Rock Hudson suffered from the disease. He died of it in October of that year.

Scientific Feuds

Emotions also ran high among scientists studying AIDS. Indeed, the AIDS epidemic in the United States was shadowed by controversy from its beginning, especially within the scientific community. Little more than a month after Heckler's triumphant announcement of Gallo's "discovery," Gallo was forced to admit that the virus he called HTLV-3 (on the assumption that it was related to two other retroviruses that he had discovered and shown to cause human blood cell cancers in the 1970s) was apparently identical to one that Luc Montagnier and his colleagues at the Pasteur Institute in France had discovered more than a year before and named LAV. Montagnier had sent a sample of this virus to Gallo's laboratory in the summer of 1983, and, after the genetic identity of LAV and HTLV-3 was discovered, the Pasteur Institute charged that Gallo's group had—accidentally or otherwise—simply reisolated Montagnier's virus.

This accusation was the start of a decade-long dispute about which man deserved credit for discovering the virus (which could have resulted in a Nobel prize), how genetically identical organisms (in a type of virus that shows considerable genetic differences from patient to patient) ended up in both laboratories, and which country should have the right to lucrative royalties from the patented blood test for the virus that grew out of the discovery. The Pasteur Institute filed a lawsuit over the patents in 1985 because, despite the fact that it had filed for a patent on the blood test before the American group, the U.S. Patent Office granted the Gallo group's request first. The suit, and the dispute, was settled at least provisionally by a historic international agreement signed in 1987 by President Ronald Reagan and French premier Jacques Chirac, who decided that their countries would share the test royalties and that the two researchers would share credit for the discovery of what came to be called HIV (human immunodeficiency virus). In 1991, however, genetic analysis conclusively proved that the virus had first come from Montagnier's laboratory. Montagnier therefore was awarded credit for having discovered HIV, although an investigation cleared Gallo of any deliberate wrongdoing. Around 2001, the researchers returned to an agreement to share credit because, although Montagnier found HIV first, Gallo was the one who provided convincing evidence that the virus caused AIDS.

Another scientific storm began in the late 1980s when a few researchers, notably Peter Duesberg, a professor of molecular and cell biology at the University of California, Berkeley, started questioning whether HIV really causes AIDS. Duesberg maintained that recreational drugs and other lifestyle factors—or even the very drugs being developed to fight AIDS—weakened the immune system enough to produce the disease. The NIH and most scientists in the field rejected Duesberg's arguments, but he later gained some powerful supporters, including Nobel prize–winner Kary Mullis.

A third scientific controversy centered on AZT (azidothymidine, also called zidovudine or Retrovir), the first drug that the federal Food and Drug Administration (FDA) approved for the treatment of AIDS (in March 1987). At first, physicians and patients alike hailed the drug as almost a miracle, but within a few years, many were complaining about AZT's side effects and noticing that it lost its effectiveness as the virus became resistant to it. Some people with AIDS, especially African Americans, even claimed that AZT was part of a government conspiracy to poison them.

A Spectrum of Reactions

Even greater controversies swirled around the ways that different segments of American society—the government, the gay community, right-wing conservatives, and the mainstream public—responded to the epidemic. For instance, AIDS activists contended that the federal government, under the control of Republican president Ronald Reagan (who refused even to utter the word *AIDS* publicly until 1987), dragged its feet on funding research on the disease. They claimed that the government refused to give AIDS the attention it deserved because Reagan's right-wing supporters strongly disapproved of homosexuals and drug users, the two groups who were initially most affected by the disease. However, supporters of the government pointed to grants given to scientists at NIH and elsewhere to study the disease in the early 1980s as evidence that the government was responding adequately.

Discussion of this issue continued in the late 1980s. Some commentators maintained that the outspoken and well-organized AIDS lobby had obtained more funds for research on the disease than Congress gave to illnesses that killed far more people, such as heart disease. Furthermore, critics said, these funds were sometimes allocated in inappropriate ways, such as focusing on the search for a cure rather than on improvements to prevention programs, which these critics felt had a better chance of controlling the epidemic. Other observers felt that an all-out attack on the disease, comparable to the American program to develop an atomic bomb during World War II, was necessary to prevent a disastrous worldwide pandemic and that Congress should therefore increase funding for AIDS research.

Gay men, individually and as a group, were torn by conflicting feelings and responses to the disaster that (in the United States, at least) had stricken them harder than anyone. Some were too beaten down with the task of caring for dying friends and lovers, grieving for the loss of hundreds of acquaintances, or even contemplating their own imminent mortality to have strength left for anything else. Others felt as much anger as grief and organized groups such as ACT UP (AIDS Coalition to Unleash Power, formed by playwright and novelist Larry Kramer in 1987) to protest what they saw as society's indifference and the slow reactions of government and science. Although many gay men, at the time and later, supported AIDS activism, the community had numerous disagreements about the form that activism should take. Some also claimed that the activists' "obsession" with AIDS distracted the community from other important issues, such as violence against homosexuals.

The public was torn between sympathy (at least for children infected at birth and "blameless victims" who had acquired the disease through blood transfusions) and fear, but fear predominated during much of the 1980s. A national poll taken in 1985 showed that 72 percent of those polled favored mandatory testing for the disease, 51 percent thought that people infected with HIV should be quarantined, and 15 percent held that such people should be tattooed so that everyone would know their condition. At one extreme of the social response were members of the conservative and religious right, who blamed promiscuous homosexuals for spreading the disease; some even claimed that AIDS was God's punishment for homosexuals' sin. At the other end of the spectrum were health care workers who tried to calm fears by educating the public about the actual risk of contracting AIDS, which was far less than most people supposed. Even some conservatives criticized the far right's stress on chastity and monogamous, heterosexual sex as the only ways to prevent the disease, claiming that such a stance was based on inaccurate or misunderstood scientific information about the way the disease was spread and unnecessarily exaggerated most people's likelihood of contracting AIDS.

Toward the end of the 1980s, the face of the AIDS epidemic and the focus of the many groups responding to it began to change as Americans came to realize that the disease was a disaster, not just in the United States but worldwide; indeed, it was affecting far more people in Africa (where it was spread primarily by heterosexual sex and by contaminated blood and needles used in medical procedures) than in North America. This planetwide threat has become the focus of most discussions about AIDS in the United States today. One hotly contested debate is over whether the United States should pay to send anti-AIDS drugs to third world countries or whether the American manufacturers of such drugs should provide them at a discount to poor countries.

The first decade of the AIDS epidemic brought out both the best and the worst in American society. It produced great acts of courage and compassion among some, such as health care workers who risked their lives to care for people with the disease before its cause and methods of spread were known. It also produced cruelties, stemming from fear, that cost many their jobs, education, or homes, and forced suffering people to die virtually alone. It made many people examine their feelings about death and about "the other"—marginalized groups from which most tried to distance themselves. It also caused rifts and raised questions, both scientific and social, that persist to this day. Examining some of the controversies of that era, which are covered in the following chapters, can produce a deeper understanding of the ways Americans—and, indeed, human beings in general—respond to disaster.

Chapter 1

Science Confronts AIDS

1

Science Views a Mystery Plague

Randy Shilts

Able to be open about their sexuality for the first time, homosexuals—mostly young, male, white, and middle class—established their own communities within certain large American cities, notably New York, San Francisco, and Los Angeles, during the 1970s. Among them was Randy Shilts, a reporter for the *San Francisco Chronicle* who came to specialize in gay issues and, eventually, the AIDS epidemic. His articles for the paper became the basis for *And the Band Played On*, his best-selling history of the early days of the epidemic, from which this selection was excerpted. In it, Shilts describes the puzzlement of the physicians who treated the first victims of the opportunistic infections, including *Pneumocystis carinii* pneumonia and the skin cancer Kaposi's sarcoma, that became hallmarks of the immune suppression produced by AIDS. In addition to *And the Band Played On*, Shilts wrote *Conduct Unbecoming: Gays and Lesbians in the U.S. Military*. Shilts died of AIDS in February 1994, at age 42.

In the United States, unexplained maladies from a mysterious new syndrome would be traced back to 1979. It was on a balmy September day in 1979 that Rick Wellikoff had been sent to Dr. Linda Laubenstein [in New York] for blood studies. She duly noted the generalized rash that resisted treatment, and the enlarged lymph nodes all over his body. Laubenstein surveyed the man and assumed he had lymph cancer. Later, a dermatologist told Linda that the man's rash was a skin cancer called Kaposi's sarcoma.

"What the hell is that?" asked Laubenstein.

It didn't take her long to find out all there was to know about it because the world's medical literature on the disease didn't take much time to read. The cancer was discovered originally among Mediterranean and Jewish men in 1871. Between 500 and 800 cases of this disease had been documented in medical books in the last century. It usually struck Jewish and Italian men in the fifth or sixth decade of their lives. In 1914, Kaposi's sarcoma, or KS, was first reported in Africa, where subsequent studies discovered that it was the most common tumor found among the Bantus, the disease generally remaining within distinct geographic boundaries in the open savannah of central Africa. There, KS patients represented one in ten cancer cases.

Typically, a victim would develop some flat, painless purple lesions and die much later, often of something else. As cancers went, Kaposi's sarcoma was fairly benign. In more recent years, reports circulated of a new, more aggressive form of the sarcoma in central Africa, but that did not appear to be what had stricken Rick Wellikoff. The lesions were not rapidly covering his body and internal organs, as had been reported among the Africans. Besides, he had never been to such exotic ports. The only characteristic that made Rick mildly different from the typical New York schoolteacher his age was that he was gay.

The only characteristic that made Rick . . . different . . . was that he was gay.

Given the rarity of the cancer—and the novelty of a case in such a young, non-Mediterranean man—Linda decided to follow Rick closely and mentioned him to several other doctors. She would have to write it up some day.

Two weeks after she first saw the schoolteacher, she got a phone call from a colleague at the Veteran's Administration Hospital, a few blocks south of New York University Medical Center on First Avenue.

"You're not going to believe it, but there's another one down here," he said.

Laubenstein quickly went to the VA Hospital to visit the other Kaposi's patient who seemed very similar to Rick. The man was much more handsome, to be sure; after all, he was a model. But he was thirty-seven years old, homosexual, and, in the strangest twist, the pair shared mutual friends. It was uncanny. Among their acquaintances, they said, was a dreamy blond flight attendant from Canada. He had an unusual name that stuck in Linda's mind.

"Gaetan. You should talk to Gaetan," the first two gay men to be diagnosed with Kaposi's sarcoma in New York City had told Linda Laubenstein in September 1979.

"You should talk to Gaetan because he's got this rash too."

October 1, 1980: Davies Medical Center, San Francisco

Michael Maletta was curt and irritated as he was being admitted to Davies Medical Center, a major medical center on Castro Street, but he had been sick all year and he wanted to get to the bottom of it. His malaise was officially described as FUO—fever of unknown origin. His doctor, however, suspected much worse and ordered up biopsies of his liver, bone marrow, and lymph nodes. Perhaps it was a Hodgkin's disease that hadn't surfaced, his internist thought. That would explain the lingering malaise that had bedeviled the hair-stylist all year. To be sure, Michael had tried to proceed with his life as normal. He still gave the best parties in town and in June had taken over all four floors of the Market Street building above his hair salon to throw the year's ultimate bash. Boys cheerfully crammed the four-story outside stairwell, swigging beers, while hundreds more squeezed into the back patios, dancing to the disco deejay. Down in the basement, scores more groped and fondled each other in a large-scale recreation of a bathhouse orgy room. And in the middle of it was Michael, the perfect host, handing out tabs of the drug MDA to all comers. These were grand times to be gay in San Francisco, Michael thought, and he relished the life-style he had built for himself since moving from Greenwich Village after the glorious Bicentennial summer. He sometimes wondered what had happened to his friends there, people like Enno Poersch and his lover Nick who had been so close. Now he wasn't hearing much from any of the old gang that had spent such hot times together in those months when the tall ships came from all over the world to New York Harbor.

University of California Medical Center, San Francisco

"Too much is being transmitted here."

It was getting to be the standard finale to Dr. Selma Dritz's rote presentation on the problem of gastrointestinal diseases among gay men. She felt her analysis had particular gravity at this monthly meeting of the sexually transmitted disease experts at the University of California at San Francisco Medical Center. This was one of the most prestigious medical schools in the nation, she knew. These doctors needed to know that something new was unfolding in the bodies of gay men, and they needed to be alert, to see where it might lead.

This was not how Dr. Dritz, the infectious disease specialist for the San Francisco Department of Public Health, had planned to spend the later years of her career—being one of the nation's foremost authorities on organisms that were setting up residence in the bowels of homosexual men. Her expertise had started soon after 1967, when she became assistant director of the San Francisco Department of Public Health's Bureau of Communicable Disease Control.

Normally, five or perhaps ten cases of amebic dysentery a year crossed her desk, and they were usually from a day-care center or restaurant. Now doctors were reporting that many a week. She checked the figures again. Nearly all the cases involved young single men, and an inordinate number were diagnosed at the Davies Medical Center on Castro Street. She mentioned to another health department staffer that it was odd because she hadn't heard any complaints about neighborhood restaurants. Her colleague took Dritz aside to explain that the cases were concentrated among gay men. Dritz didn't understand the relevance of the observation.

"It's oral-anal contact," he said.

"It's what?"

They didn't teach these things when Selma was in medical school in the 1940s, but she quickly learned the down-and-dirty realities about enteric diseases. Gay doctors had long recognized that parasitic diseases like amebiasis, giardiasis, and shigellosis were simply a health hazard of being gay. The problems grew with the new popularity of anal sex, in the late 1960s and early 1970s, because it was nearly impossible to avoid contact with fecal matter during that act.

As sexual tastes grew more exotic and rimming became fashionable, the problem exploded. There wasn't a much more efficient way to get a dose of parasite spoor than by such direct ingestion.

Although all this was common knowledge among gay physicians, the awareness had evaded the public health profession. Earnest health officials at one point dispatched inspectors to Greenwich Village to test water after detecting unusual outbreaks of amoebas in the neighborhood.

The more expert Dritz became about the health problems of the gay community, however, the more concerned she grew. Gay men were being washed by tide after tide of increasingly serious infections. First it was syphilis and gonorrhea. Gay men made up about 80 percent of the 70,000 annual patient visits to the city's VD [venereal, or sexually transmitted, disease] clinic. Easy treatment had imbued them with such a cavalier attitude toward venereal diseases that many gay men saved their waiting-line numbers, like little tokens of desirability, and the clinic was considered an easy place to pick up both a shot and a date. Then came hepatitis A and the enteric parasites, followed by the proliferation of hepatitis B, a disease that had transformed itself, via the popularity of anal intercourse, from a blood-borne scourge into a venereal disease.

"Too much is being transmitted here."

Dritz was nothing if not cool and businesslike. Being emotional got in the way of getting her message across, of making a difference. Her calm admonitions to gay men about the dangers of rimming and unprotected anal sex were well rehearsed by now, although they were out of beat with that era. The sheer weight of her professionalism, however, made Dritz immensely popular among gay doctors. Her children teased her that she was the "sex queen of San Francisco" and the "den mother of the gays." Gay health had become an area in which Dritz had an unparalleled expertise because she had spent much of the late 1970s meeting with gay doctors, penning medical journal articles, and traveling around northern California to issue her no-nonsense health warnings.

But here, in 1980, among these venereal disease specialists, Dritz found her message received cooly, at best. She recognized the response. Scientists had a hard time believing that the sexual revolution had turned Montezuma's revenge and hepatitis B, the junkies' malady, into a social disease. Dritz calmly repeated the statistics: Between 1976 and 1980, shigellosis had increased 700 percent among single men in their thirties. Only seventeen cases of amebiasis were reported in 1969; now the reported cases, which were only a small portion of the city's true caseload, were well past 1,000 a year. Cases of hepatitis B among men in their thirties had quadrupled in the past four years.

These diseases were particularly difficult to fight because they all had latent periods in which they showed no symptoms even while the carrier was infectious—gay men were spreading the disease to countless others long before they knew they themselves were sick. This was a scenario for catastrophe, Dritz thought, and the commercialization of promiscuity in bathhouses was making it worse.

Dritz looked down from her slide projector to the disbelieving faces in the conference room. These med-school types didn't believe anything unless they saw it in their microscopes or test tubes, she thought. This, they argued, was "anecdotal" information and they needed data. All this talk about buggery and oral-anal contact didn't make them any more comfortable either.

Dritz tried to broaden her point, so the doctors could see that she wasn't talking so much about this or that disease, or specific sexual gymnastics.

"Too much is being transmitted," she said. "We've got all these diseases going unchecked. There are so many opportunities for transmission that, if something new gets loose here, we're going to have hell to pay.". . .

November 1980: University of California, Los Angeles

Finally, something interesting.

Dr. Michael Gottlieb's four-month career as an assistant professor at UCLA had proved anything but scintillating. Fresh from his training at Stanford, the thirty-two-year-old immunologist had done what ambitious young scientists are supposed to do when they get their first job at a prestigious medical research center: He went to work with mice. Gottlieb had dutifully brought his own mice from Stanford to

UCLA and planned to study the effects of radiation on their immune system, but the damned rodents kept dropping dead from viruses they had picked up in Los Angeles. Gottlieb wasn't terribly enthralled by bench work [laboratory work] anyway, so he put out the word that his residents should beat the bushes for something interesting—some patient that might teach them a thing or two about the immune system.

"If something new gets loose here, we're going to have hell to pay."

It didn't take long for an eager young resident to come back with the story of a young man who was suffering from a yeast infection in his throat that was so severe he could hardly breathe. Babies born with defects in their immune systems sometimes suffered from this florid candidiasis, as would a cancer patient who had been loaded down with chemotherapy, Gottlieb knew, but he'd never seen such a thing in a thirty-one-year-old who appeared perfectly healthy in other respects.

Gottlieb and his residents examined the young man and collectively scratched their heads.

Two days later, the patient, an artist, complained of shortness of breath. He had also developed a slight cough. On a hunch, Gottlieb twisted some arms to convince pathologists to take a small scraping of the patient's lung tissue through a nonsurgical maneuver. The results presented young Doctor Gottlieb with the strangest array of symptoms he'd ever heard of—the guy had *Pneumocystis carinii* pneumonia.

Gottlieb walked a tube of blood down the hall to a lab immunologist who, like himself, was always on the lookout for something that broke the routine. This researcher was specializing in the new science of T-cells, the recently discovered white blood cells that are key components of the immune system. Gottlieb asked for a T-cell count on the patient. There are two kinds of T-lymphocyte cells to look for: T-helper cells that activate the specific disease-fighting cells and give chemical instructions for creating the antibodies that destroy microbial invaders, and the T-suppressor cells that tell the immune system when the threat ended. The colleague ran his tests on the patient's blood, laboriously hand-counting the subgroups of T-cells. He was floored by the outcome: There weren't any T-helper cells. Figuring he had made a mistake, he tested the blood again, with the same results.

Hot damn. What kind of disease tracked down and killed such specific blood cells? Gottlieb brainstormed with residents, colleagues, and anyone with a spare hour. Nobody had a clue. Now Gottlieb was excited. He pored over his books and tracked down research on obscure immunological diseases. Nothing explained it. He also examined the minutiae of the artist's medical charts; he had suffered from a cornucopia of venereal diseases. In a conversation, the patient mentioned that he was gay, but Gottlieb didn't think any more of that than the fact the guy might drive a Ford.

After weeks of fruitless investigation, Gottlieb was still stumped. Maybe some leukemia would surface later on. In a year or two, he thought, we'll find out what's wrong.

2

Robert C. Gallo Discovered the Cause of AIDS

Robert C. Gallo

In 1981, Robert C. Gallo was head of the Laboratory of Tumor Cell Biology at the National Cancer Institute, part of the National Institutes of Health, a group of large, federally funded medical research institutions in Bethesda, Maryland. (He now directs the Institute of Human Virology at the University of Maryland in Baltimore.) At that time, Gallo had already become famous for discovering the first viruses shown to cause cancer in humans. These viruses, called HTLV-1 and HTLV-2, belonged to an unusual group called retroviruses, which can insert their genes directly into the genome (collection of genes) of the cells they infect. The HTLVs attacked CD4 T cells, a type of immune system cell found in the blood, and made them turn cancerous. Gallo and others had found that the viruses could be spread through blood transfusions and by sexual contact.

As Gallo recounts in this selection from his autobiography, *Virus Hunting*, when he first heard about the syndrome affecting young gay men in late 1981 and early 1982, he was struck by the fact that it, too, seemed to be spread by sex and blood and produced damage to T cells, resulting in destruction of the immune system. He began to suspect that the illness might be caused by another member of the HTLV family. After some initial hesitation, his laboratory set out to find the new virus. Gallo and his colleagues succeeded, after many difficulties, in isolating the virus (which Gallo dubbed HTLV-3) and showing that it was strongly associated with the disease by then called AIDS. They prepared a blood test to identify antibodies to the virus, which would indicate exposure. Secretary of Health and Human Services Margaret Heckler announced

Excerpted from *Virus Hunting: AIDS, Cancer, and the Human Retrovirus: A Story of Scientific Discovery*, by Robert C. Gallo (New York: BasicBooks, 1991).

these discoveries with great fanfare on April 23, 1984, but Gallo soon found himself embroiled in controversy.

The first medical account I heard of the disease that came to be called AIDS came in the summer of 1981, at the University of California, Los Angeles (UCLA). Michael Gottlieb and his co-workers reported a cluster of pneumonia cases in young male homosexuals in Los Angeles caused by a protozoan parasite known as *Pneumocystis carinii* (PC), a common but normally not pathogenic microbe. Previously, PC was found to have caused pneumonia only rarely, and then in severely immune-depressed people. It had been observed, for example, in those whose immune systems had been intentionally weakened by medical therapy as part of the preparation for organ transplantation.

Almost at the same time, Alvin Friedman-Kien and coworkers at New York University Medical School found a cluster of previously quite rare Kaposi's sarcoma (KS) cases among homosexuals, and a similar cluster of disease in gay men in New York was reported by Fred Siegel and coworkers at Mt. Sinai School of Medicine in New York. The Kaposi's sarcoma disease showed up as purple, cancer-like lesions of the skin. Still other clinicians began to report lymph gland enlargement in young male homosexuals, as well as an odd increase in an unusual B-cell lymphoma (a cancer of the lymph glands of B-cell type). . . .

These extraordinary findings did not go unnoticed by the Centers for Disease Control (CDC) in Atlanta, whose role it is to monitor disease patterns. James Curran at the CDC and a few other epidemiologists believed they might be looking at the first signs of a newly emerging and potentially epidemic disease. I soon became aware that clinicians were reporting another unusual finding, one that would prove particularly intriguing: young male patients with a reduced number of circulating T-cells and in particular a reduction chiefly in the T-cells known as T4 lymphocytes or the $CD4^+$ T-cells.[1]

1. T4-cells are now usually called $CD4^+$ T-cells by medical scientists. Thus, the terms T4 and CD4 can be used interchangeably. CD4 is a specific protein molecule on the surface of some mature T-cells. It has an important function: it helps "bridge" the T4-cell to some other cell types (like macrophages) by its loosely binding to a specific protein on the surface of those cells. This helps the two cells exchange signals during the immune response.

Defining a New Disease

In late 1981 Curran came over to the National Institutes of Health (NIH) to talk about these new epidemiological findings. His purpose was not simply informational. If all this confusing data were in fact defining a new disease, and if the disease were as serious as he suspected, it would be necessary to get NIH talent working on it. But who could make the most useful contribution: researchers in infectious disease, virologists, oncologists, immunologists?

Curran provided us with a description of what he considered the range of sexual practices between males—not for voyeuristic reasons, but because of the possibility that hidden within their patterns of sexual activity might be a clue to understanding the disease. The early epidemiological findings pointed to some connection between male homosexuality and the disease, though no one yet understood just how any of the sexual practices of gays—either the type of practices or the frequency of contact—could contribute to the cause or spread of the disease, if indeed they contributed to either. Though no one who heard Curran speak or followed reports in the press could fail to be moved by the horror of what this new disease was doing to young male homosexuals, nothing Curran said that day caused me to believe that this was an area of research our lab should move into.

But Curran returned in early 1982 with far more—and far more compelling—epidemiological information. If my memory is correct, it was at this time that I learned there was reason to believe that the disease was showing up in people who had had blood transfusions, implying a microbial agent. As well, there was by now clear evidence that it compromised T-cell function, an area of study closely related to our work on HTLV.

Many of the theories about how the disease was spread—ranging from the reasonable but unimaginative, to the questionable but creative, to the outright bizarre—did not presume an infectious origin. Yet Curran seemed nearly convinced that an infectious agent was involved, probably a new one. He had no data suggesting what the agent might be, or be like, and never speculated in this direction, but here is where he thought we ought to start looking, and start fast.

This second talk did shake me up and led me to think very carefully about AIDS. Frankly, it is my belief that Curran's efforts and those of a few others through this period, including Dean Mann at the National Cancer Institute

(NCI) and Bob Redfield at Walter Reed Hospital, were central to the first appreciation of the AIDS problem by much of the medical world. I shudder to think what might have occurred had they and others not forced what turned out to be an eleventh-hour warning on a research community that sometimes sees itself as too tied up with previous research commitments to undertake new ones.

An Altered Virus

I left Curran's conference stimulated and concerned. Of greatest interest to me was that this new disease, likely infectious and threatening to become an epidemic, appeared to involve T4-cells, those white blood cells of the lymphocyte lineage. The precise method of transmission in gay men had not been established, but the vehicle of transmission in all other cases seemed to be blood. Later we would learn that it was also transmitted from mother to fetus (or mother to child, if the infection occurred during the birth process). Shortly thereafter I happened to speak with my collaborator Max Essex, who reminded me of several important studies that had shown a correlation between some animal retroviruses and the suppression of the immune system. William Jarrett, for example, had observed more than a decade earlier that the feline leukemia retrovirus more often caused an AIDS-like immune deficiency in cats than it did leukemia. Max had confirmed and recently extended these results, and we wondered aloud whether the disease in cats might be caused by a small mutation in the genome of the feline leukemia virus.[2]

Essex had also told me about his recent study in Japan showing that there were more HTLV-1-positive people in infectious disease wards than in other medical wards. Conversely, research by Takatsuki found more opportunistic infections in leukemic patients infected with HTLV-1 than one would expect. And several labs—including mine (with my co-workers Marv Reitz and Mika Popovic); David Folkman and Tony Fauci at NIH; Bo DuPont at Sloan-Kettering Institute in New York; and Nicole Suciu-Foca at Columbia—had published evidence that HTLV-1 could be immunosuppressive *in vitro:* that is, it could harm the func-

2. In 1987 we learned from the work of James Mullins that this is almost exactly the case. Certain changes in the envelope of the cat leukemia virus convert it into a virus that can cause an AIDS-like disease.

tion of T-cells in laboratory cultures.

I started reviewing all we knew about HTLV in the new light of what we were learning about this new disease. The HTLVs were transmitted by blood and sex, as well as gestation, the birth process, and mother's milk. HTLVs infected T4 lymphocytes and could reduce the immune function of T4-cells. Was AIDS caused by a retrovirus? Was this retrovirus in fact a variant of HTLV-1 (or 2)? Was it perhaps a new retrovirus—one related to the HTLVs?

Findings pointed to some connection between male homosexuality and the disease.

Intellectually, I began to play out one scenario. What if AIDS were due to a mutation of an HTLV, probably occurring in Africa, which had spread to Haiti, then to the United States? The feline leukemia virus (FELV) mutation idea, if proved correct, should make us think about a similar possibility with the HTLVs—if, in fact, the causative agent did turn out to be a retrovirus. Perhaps the differences between the way an HTLV caused T-cell leukemia and the way a related retrovirus caused AIDS might be due to a small change in those extra regulatory genes (called now *tax* and *rex*) that Yoshida in Japan, the Harvard group, [Flossie] Wong-Staal and others in our group, and later other groups had found in the HTLVs but that were not known in any animal viruses. Or perhaps a change had occurred in the envelope by some mutation or other means of genetic alteration. Differences in the envelopes of various strains of the same animal retrovirus can lead that virus to cause different diseases. A lot of ifs, but that's how we decided where to start to look for confirmation of an idea.

A Dangerous Project

But at first I hesitated to plunge in. Looking back, I see clearly now that part of what was holding me back was the memory of how much trouble we had had getting the scientific community to accept the existence of even one human retrovirus. Now we had two—HTLV-1 and HTLV-2—and there was still plenty of work to be done on them. It was tempting simply to continue with that work now that it was going well. I decided to sound out an old friend, a bit of a tough egg who had more experience than I in the scientific life.

Sometime in early 1982 I met my close friend, the late GianPiero DiMayorca, for dinner in Bethesda [Maryland]. Born and raised in Milan, DiMayorca was a highly intelligent, handsome, brash, but very—perhaps too—cynical virologist. In the early 1980s he became chairman of microbiology at the New Jersey School of Medicine and Dentistry in Newark.

By all accounts, he argued, AIDS was a dreadful disease; if it followed the pattern of past epidemic diseases, it might be years, maybe centuries, before a cure for it would be found. If it turned out to be infectious, which seemed more certain every day, how infectious would it be, how ingenious its agent of infection in getting around the defenses that had evolved—both physiologically and culturally—to help us deal with other dangerous microbes? And what special risks would there be in studying the illness and in handling specimens?

[The disease] seemed to be killing everyone who came down with it.

Despite the extreme caution that is part of the environment of any good lab, my friend pointed out, other microbes had in the recent past infected laboratory workers attempting to isolate them. He mentioned Marburg virus and other instances where an unknown agent had been brought into a laboratory and had harmed or killed virologists or their technical staff.[3]

There was a further frightening aspect to this new disease. It appeared, so far, that no one spontaneously recovered from it. It did not run its course over a short period of time, reach a critical stage, and then either kill the patient or leave him or her recovered with some natural immunity to new infection. It seemed to be killing everyone who came down with it. If I brought it into my lab, I risked not only my own life but the lives of my co-workers. I might be

3. Marburg virus belongs to a new class of RNA viruses. It was discovered in 1967 after an outbreak in Europe in which thirty-one people were infected and seven died. It began when virus from African green monkeys infected laboratory scientists who were working with the monkeys' kidneys.

spending the next decade or so watching one former colleague after another come down with those first symptoms that would mark him or her as having contracted a surely fatal disease.

Having put these ghoulish thoughts into my head, DiMayorca then turned toward the professional aspect of doing research on AIDS. Patients with AIDS, he reminded me, were infected with so many different microbes (either because of lifestyle or because of the suppression of their immune systems) that establishing any one agent as the sole cause could prove frustrating, perhaps impossible. In short, the whole dangerous project showed slim prospects for professional success when measured against its downside.

"If you are right about the retrovirus idea," DiMayorca said to me, "let someone else do the dangerous work. You can sit back and watch, knowing you and your staff originated the notion and already found the first human retroviruses. If you are wrong, you have much to lose; if correct, little to gain. Let them turn to you and your group as experienced advisers. Your people have earned this. Also, you are a cancer researcher in the National Cancer Institute. This new epidemic is not a priority for cancer research, even though Kaposi's sarcoma appears to be a part of it. At least it's not a priority yet."

The Start of a Long Road

Neither my friend nor I considered at the time the possibility that did come to pass—that I would fully embrace work on AIDS, that I would turn out to be, in the main, right, and that my reputation would still suffer. Ours would become the most influential lab in the AIDS field, putting itself out front on the retrovirus theory; we would turn out to be dead right about a retrovirus being the culprit; we would contribute substantially to the identification and culturing of the particular retrovirus that causes AIDS; we would be the first to grow the AIDS virus in sufficient quantities to begin serious work with it; we would be the first to develop a workable blood-screening test for AIDS; we would produce much of the information on the basic makeup of the virus; we would provide most of the results that showed the new virus to be the cause of AIDS; we would begin to understand the relationship between AIDS infection and the more aggressive form of Kaposi's sarcoma; we would discover a new herpes virus as a possible co-factor. And yet despite all this hard work, by myself and my colleagues, I would find my reputation attacked in the press coverage of a patent suit between the United States and French governments—a lawsuit, I might add, to which I was not a party, over a patent I had not requested and from which I never expected any financial gain.

Ultimately, the suggestion would be made (and at times mindlessly repeated, until responsible people who should have known better would demand an investigation of me because of it) that the Pasteur Institute in Paris had done all the work and that the Laboratory of Tumor Cell Biology had either misappropriated or somehow stolen their AIDS virus.

Of course, in 1982, I had no crystal ball and had to go with my feelings. DiMayorca's arguments were not without basis, but even before I met with him I had already decided to devote at least some lab time to AIDS research. Curran had caught my attention. Citing the earliest epidemiologic findings of the CDC, he put forth the idea that this seemingly random collection of symptoms, which was still being characterized as a syndrome, would turn out to be a single disease with a single cause. In making this prediction, he and a few others would be correct and way ahead of most others then thinking about AIDS. For myself, of greatest importance was that I suspected he was right. Within a short period of time, I would be prepared to go a step farther and suggest that the agent most likely responsible for this disease was a virus, and more specifically a retrovirus. At our next staff meeting, I suggested that a few in the lab get tissue and begin cell culturing while others might want to do molecular analyses of DNA obtained directly from tissue of AIDS patients—using probes from the HTLVs to see whether we could find sequences [DNA fragments] related to an HTLV.[4] No one demurred.

And so we began.

4. Molecular probes, in this case, are segments of the DNA proviral genes of the HTLVs tested with DNA from AIDS patients' blood cells and from Kaposi's sarcoma tissue for the interaction known as molecular hybridization. A positive result means that in some cells a virus is present.

Luc Montagnier Discovered the Cause of AIDS

Luc Montagnier

Like Robert Gallo's research group at the National Institutes of Health, Luc Montagnier and his colleagues at the Pasteur Institute in Paris, France, were trying to identify the cause of AIDS. In early 1983, Montagnier's group isolated a virus that they called LAV from the cells of an AIDS patient. While continuing to work on it themselves, they shared samples of the virus with Gallo's laboratory in the summer of 1983. After Gallo announced his discovery of the virus he called HTLV-3 in April 1984, the Pasteur Institute insisted that Gallo—accidentally or otherwise—had simply reisolated LAV.

In this excerpt from his autobiography, *Virus*, Montagnier describes the growing ill will between himself and Gallo during 1983 and 1984 and his feeling that the Pasteur Institute team's discoveries were slighted, not only in the United States but in France as well. He claims that Gallo refused to recognize differences between the new virus that both groups isolated and HTLV, the cancer-causing virus that Gallo had identified earlier. Later, Montagnier says, Gallo refused to acknowledge the similarity between LAV and HTLV-3.

The dispute between Montagnier's and Gallo's laboratories that began at this time would last for decades and come to involve a lawsuit and an agreement signed by the leaders of their respective countries. Around 2001, the two researchers finally agreed to share credit for the discovery of the AIDS virus, which was eventually named HIV. Montagnier was

Excerpted from *Virus: The Co-Discoverer of HIV Tracks Its Rampage and Charts the Future*, by Luc Montagnier (New York: W.W. Norton & Company, 2000).

shown to have found the virus first, but Gallo was the one who linked it clearly to AIDS. Montagnier and Gallo are now collaborating in attempts to develop an AIDS vaccine.

In June 1983, I met with [American AIDS researcher] Robert Gallo in Paris, at the apartment of a mutual friend, Guy de Thé. Then we had dinner in a fish restaurant on the Left Bank. The discussion quickly heated up. I presented one argument after another. Gallo would have none of them: he maintained that LAV was a variant of HTLV. I believe that at the time he was unfamiliar with lentiviruses ["slow viruses," a family of viruses to which Montagnier thought LAV belonged] and more importantly, that he could not imagine that two so distinct families of retrovirus were capable of attacking humans. However, he invited me to take part in a meeting of a task force he had put together at the National Institutes of Health (NIH), and asked me to bring a specimen of LAV so that his collaborators could analyze it.

And so in early July I was on my way to Gallo's house, located in Bethesda, Maryland, not far from the NIH, with a specimen of LAV frozen in dry ice. It was a Sunday, and it was hot. I briefly joined a game of handball nearing its end in Gallo's garden, once the specimen had been placed in a domestic freezer at -20°C. The next day, the meeting was a festival for HTLV. I was given barely a few minutes to speak about LAV and show the photographs taken with the electron microscope. I made it clear in my report that LAV was very different from HTLV, that it was more like a slow virus, the infectious equine [horse] anemia virus. I think only Matthew Gonda, the microscopist working with Gallo, remarked that these images were indeed those of a slow virus and understood the importance of this similarity with animal lentiviruses. The report of the meeting, drawn up by Gallo's secretaries, barely mentions my talk and alludes only in passing to a virus isolated in France, to which he gives the name HTLV-III.

Before leaving France, I had had a proposal for collaboration between the NIH and the Pasteur Institute drawn up by Danielle Bernemann, head of the Industrial Property Department of our institute. At her request, we had then immediately deposited our main isolates of virus at the National Collection of Microorganism Cultures (CNCM). I had brought a copy of the collaboration plan with me to Bethesda. However, after the meeting, I was overcome with exasperation that no attention had really been paid to our new virus. Now there was no longer any question of working together on these terms. When I got back to the Pasteur Institute, I was more determined than ever to continue along the path we were on.

Indeed, with the summer came even more proof in our favor. We isolated LAV from the blood of a young hemophiliac stricken with AIDS. He had a brother who was also infected but still in good condition. Both of them, suffering from hemophilia B, had received blood products (factor IX) prepared by the French National Center of Blood Transfusions (CNTS). But during a vacation in Austria, they had also received preparations made with American plasma, and thus the origin of their contamination remained undetermined.

I was overcome with exasperation that no attention had really been paid to our new virus.

The first epidemiological studies (which seek to determine the prevalence of a disease in a community) were conducted in our laboratory by Françoise Brun-Vézinet and Christine Rouzioux with the help of the very first ELISA (enzyme-linked immunosorbent assay) tests. These showed that most patients suffering from lymphadenopathy had antibodies against the virus LAV and were therefore infected by the same type of virus. In any case, we had enough information to take action and present our case to the authorities and the scientific community.

Urgent Letters

In August 1983, I sent a series of letters, almost identical in content, to the competent French authorities: the director general of the National Center for Scientific Research (CNRS), the director general of INSERM (National Institute of Medical Research), the director general of Health, and the director of research at the Ministry of Research. In these letters I said:

> Recent findings indicate that a young hemophiliac stricken with AIDS has been infected with the LAV [HIV] virus. The cause of infection was most probably the antihemophilic concentrates he receives regularly. These fragmentary data authorize me to consider this virus potentially dangerous to humans and to alert the relevant authorities to the national benefit that would be gained by very quickly developing the means to diagnose and prevent the dissemination of this virus, since we cannot exclude the possibility of its spread through blood products.

I also wrote to Professor Soulié, director of the CNTS (National Center of Blood Transfusions), to inform him of the need to heat antihemophilic products.

These letters received almost nothing more than polite replies, with the exception of a visit from two colléagues close to the decision-making process, Jean-Paul Lévy and Jean-François Bach, and the allocation of 500,000 francs from the Ministry of Research. This was not enough to construct a P_3 [BL_3] laboratory [a laboratory constructed with the highest level of protection against the spread of dangerous microorganisms], the kind of security laboratory needed to safely produce the virus in mass quantities.

Why all the fuss over the hundred or so cases of AIDS recorded in France, the great majority of which were homosexuals? That was not a problem of public health. What's more, our findings might even not be true, since they were not consistent with the Americans' findings. Only a Charles de Gaulle, at the political level, or a Jacques Monod [former head of the Pasteur Institute], at the scientific level, could have understood and taken the necessary steps to quickly expand our research and develop a blood test. But these two were no longer with us.

Harsh Questioning

As for the specialists, their response was no better. I was invited by Gallo to a colloquium on retroviruses which James Watson had asked him to organize at Cold Spring Harbor, together with Max Essex and Ludwig Gross, the discoverer of the first mouse leukemia retrovirus. Cold Spring Harbor Laboratory, on Long Island, New York, is the Mecca for molecular biologists: James Watson, one of the "fathers" of the double helix [codiscoverer of the structure of DNA], developed molecular biology laboratories there and made the place into an incomparable conference center. The colloquium focused on HTLV and leukemia: only one session, the last, would deal with AIDS. The date was September 15, 1983. Many of the participants had already left; I spoke to a half-empty hall. Moreover, the chairman of the session, Don Francis of the U.S. Centers for Disease Control and Prevention (CDC), seemed anxious to conclude and granted me no grace period beyond the twenty-minute limit. A barrage of questions followed my presentation, some of them honest, some of them less so: Was I really sure it was a retrovirus? Did we really observe reverse transcriptase activity? Guy de Thé himself told me he was convinced we had found a new retrovirus. But he expressed his reservations as to its causal role. As for Gallo, I asked him to explain the reason for his position, while he had all the details of our work in his hands in the form of my manuscript. "You punched me out," he said. That is, I had demolished all his work on HTLV and AIDS. And yet, in the conclusion of my report, in an attempt to be open-minded, I did not rule out HTLV either. I had naively believed I would convince the doubters, whereas I was up against a wall of indifference and bad faith.

I was up against a wall of indifference and bad faith.

Before returning to Paris I gave a speech in New York, at the Rockefeller University. The attendees listened to me politely, nothing more. On my way back, I had planned to give a press conference as well as an interview. The interview was to be conducted by John Maurice, a journalist who had talked about LAV (and HTLV) in the *Journal of the American Medical Association (JAMA)*. I canceled the interview, and the Pasteur Institute management, in agreement with the CNRS, asked me to cancel my press conference scheduled for Paris as well, in lieu of which they published a simple press release. But still another disappointment awaited me. David Klatzmann had drafted an article on the virus's tropism for (attraction to) T_4 [CD4] lymphocytes, which he had submitted for publication to *Nature*. The journal turned it down. One of the experts consulted denied the human origin of LAV: was it not a laboratory contaminant originating in a mouse virus? And yet we knew this was impossible, since the patient had antibodies against his own virus. In addition, this expert rather elegantly advised us to wait for two years before publishing our report, "as Robert Gallo would have done for HTLV." No doubt this English consultant was close to HTLV supporters. Despite our protests, our replies, our explanations, there was no appealing this decision, a strangely hostile stance for a high-level scientific journal toward a rather extraordinary discovery.

Rejected Articles

In anger, I sent to the *Nature* editor a copy of the manuscript I had presented at Cold Spring for publication in the book of the conference, which was supposed to be published in January 1984. In fact I was one of the few to turn in my manuscript before the deadline. The book would not be published until June 1984, and would contain a few chapters on Gallo's new HTLV-III virus (identical to LAV) written in 1984, well after the conference. As for the article on T_4 tropism, which was important in proving the role of LAV in AIDS, it was to suffer an even more sinister fate. After it was turned down by *Nature*, Jean-Claude Gluckman and Klatzmann rewrote it and sent it to another high-level journal, the American *Proceedings of the National Academy of Science (PNAS)*. The paper first had to be presented to *PNAS* by a member of the academy, who would select two experts to review it. André Lwoff, a renowned Pasteurian, agreed to present the article, and I proposed to him a list of possible experts. One of them never even sent back his opinion, as though he had never received the manuscript, and Lwoff did not dare send it to another expert. Finally, in the spring of 1984, we sent it to *Science*. Gallo's articles on HTLV-III had already appeared, and Ruth Kulstadt, one of the *Science* editors, told us she would be interested in articles by the French group. Klatzmann and Gluckman rewrote it a third time—overnight—and the new version was published in July 1984, almost a year after the initial submission to *Nature!*

Meanwhile, an article I had sent to *Science* on the similarity between LAV and the horse anemia virus did not enjoy a better fate. I finally published it in March 1984 in the annals of the Pasteur Institute. I still retain—and I think the same is true for associates and colleagues—a feeling of bitterness about this period. We knew we were right, but we were the only ones. Many discoverers must have had the same experience, but this time it was a question of public health. I have often wondered if there was any way things could have happened differently. Perhaps we should have immediately published our findings in French-language journals such as *Les Comptes rendus de l'Académie des sciences* (Reviews of the Academy of Sciences) and alerted the press. But I am not entirely convinced. The French virological community was itself resigned to seeing the light come only from across the Atlantic. Even Jacques Leibowitch, so far ahead of the rest in promoting the notion of a retrovirus, never got past HTLV and even as late as March 1984 published a book entitled *Un Virus venu d'ailleurs* (A virus from elsewhere), in which HTLV is presented as the cause of AIDS and LAV is accorded but a single paragraph. As for the press, the newspapers that set the tone, such as *Le Monde*, were leaning toward Robert Gallo, despite having published one of the first articles favorable to the LAV thesis, written by its medical writer Jean-Yves Nau, who was harshly criticized for it. A conference organized in Paris in October 1983 by the Association pour la Recherche sur le Cancer (Association for Cancer Research) (ARC) pitted me against Gallo. I presented the initial results of the ELISA test and announced that the test would be marketed by IPP [the Pasteur Institute of Production which manufactures and markets vaccine's and tests made by the Pasteur Institute]. My American colleague then stood up to warn IPP and the French authorities against such a venture. It was the same story at a meeting organized by INSERM at Seillac, in the Loire Valley: even French "experts" in electron microscopy cast doubt on the retroviral nature of LAV. I guess it is the fate of pioneers never to be understood right away! But this sort of ignorance—mere stupidity or bad faith?—was to cause delays in developing the detection test, which would have deadly consequences for hemophiliacs and transfusion recipients. Fortunately, a few months later, the wind was to change direction.

A More Vigorous Virus

Meanwhile findings continued to come in from our laboratory. The initial BRU virus was changing upon serial passages (growth from generation to generation) in lymphocyte cultures. It had become fatal to lymphocytes in culture. In October, with my late lamented colleague Jacqueline Gruest, I discovered a new property of the virus, one that we had looked for in vain upon first isolating it: it multiplied in continuous lines of tumor cells. These were not T_4 lines, but rather antibody-producing cells (B lymphocytes) that had been either immortalized by the Epstein-Barr virus (EBV, an infectious agent of the herpes group) or taken from Burkitt's lymphomas (lymph tumors found in African children). This discovery ensured a better production of virus.

We knew we were right, but we were the only ones.

We ascribed these changes to the long stretches of time spent in vitro by the BRU virus. In particular, the Klatzmann-Gluckman group and Chermann had tried to infect some precursors of T lymphocytes present in the bone marrow. The experiment proved inconclusive, but the virus that was propagated in this fashion seemed to have given birth to a livelier, more virulent variant, called MT. It was this MT virus that I used in the experiments with the lines of B lymphocytes. Also, in September 1983, despite the growing mistrust that was beginning to come between us and Robert Gallo, we once again sent him, at his request, two specimens of virus, one of which was MT. The July specimen, by his account, would not grow in his laboratory. We now know—having only found out in 1991—that this MT virus was not BRU's, but came from the patient LAI. Was this due to a labeling error, an accidental mix-up that occurred when the BRU, LAI, and LOI viruses were all grown in culture at the same time for the production of the ELISA test? It is important to understand that when an infectious agent reproduces faster than others, even if it is initially present in a smaller quantity, it can quickly replace the other variants. Whatever the case, the BRU/MT/LAI virus had contaminated the local viral strains of several outside laboratories, including Gallo's in the United States, and that of Robin Weiss, a well-known retrovirus specialist in London.

In February 1984, Chermann and Brun-Vézinet left for Park City, Utah, where one of the multiple conferences organized each winter by the University of California, Los

Angeles (UCLA) is held. Chermann presented all of our findings on AIDS, while Gallo publicly stuck to his position regarding HTLV. Many things were happening in his laboratory—as we were to find out later. Mika Popovic, a Slovak researcher who had worked on retroviruses at Bratislava, had rejoined Gallo's team. He was the one in charge of all the HTLV-I cultures. In autumn of 1983, he succeeded in making our MT virus grow on lines of T_4 tumor cells. He was about to characterize it and notified Robert Gallo of this, but was told to keep silent. When, in December, Popovic called me to ask for some anti-interferon serum, he was careful not to tell me that he had learned how to cultivate our virus on a continuous cell line, and only laconically remarked: "I know how to grow your virus."

Identical Viruses

Chermann was given a better reception at Park City than I had received at Cold Spring Harbor. The CDC researchers, especially Don Francis, were more open this time and recognized the validity of our work. The research on HTLV was going nowhere, while our work was making progress. The LAV ELISA test, thanks to the virus produced on continuous cell lines, was of a high quality.

In late March of 1984, Robert Gallo telephoned me to say he had isolated a new virus that was growing very well, an HTLV a bit different from the others that he called HTLV-III. In his opinion, it was the AIDS agent. Had he compared it with LAV? I asked. I could not hear the answer. A few days later at the beginning of April, he came to Paris. Chermann had invited him, along with several CDC researchers, including Francis, to give a series of lectures to French scientists on the retroviral origin of AIDS. Gallo refused to talk about HTLV-III in public, as his findings were to be published in *Science* in early May. But in private he agreed to give us a few details. Francis wanted to be present at this meeting. He too had isolated a virus comparable to ours, at the CDC in Atlanta. But Gallo refused to speak about HTLV-III with him present: one more virus is meaningless, compared to his own forty-eight isolates, he said. I was very troubled by this reaction, which was rather discourteous, to say the least. Finally, Francis agreed to leave the room, while the three of us—Chermann, Barré-Sinoussi, and myself—remained with Gallo. The latter repeated that he had not compared his new virus to LAV, but said he was ready to do this in a collaboration whose findings would be made known worldwide. Moreover, his findings would be presented at a press conference, although the time and place of the announcement were no longer his to decide, but the U.S. government's.

We were satisfied, since the HTLV-III virus Gallo described to us resembled LAV/MT like an identical twin. But we were also disappointed, since ethically speaking he ought to have already compared it with the virus we had sent to him, and if identical, should not have changed its name. This is my main criticism of Robert Gallo. He later acknowledged his mistake in private conversations, and believes he has paid dearly for it. Especially as his most famous isolate, HTLV-IIIB—the one which has been used in all American blood detection tests—has proved to be but a contamination of the Pasteur virus LAV/MT[2] (in fact, LAI). But let's not get ahead of ourselves . . .

The press conference was held on April 28, 1984 in Washington, D.C. Gallo, sounding very tense, telephoned me before and after the event. I advised him to make sure to mention the work we at Pasteur had done. In fact, the press conference, as it was reported on the teletypes and later over the radio, proclaimed a great victory for American science. The Secretary of the U.S. Department of Health and Human Services, Margaret Heckler, lost her voice at an unfortunate moment, preventing her from reading the paragraph that was supposed to give credit to the work of the Pasteur team. Even after fifteen years these events still leave a bitter taste in my mouth, even though I am aware that the extraordinary publicity Gallo rallied around his virus reflected onto ours. For the entire scientific community, in any case, the cause was now understood: LAV/HTLV-III was indeed the cause of AIDS, period.

HIV Does Not Cause AIDS

Peter H. Duesberg

Although most scientists accepted the claim that the virus that came to be called HIV (Human Immunodeficiency Virus) causes AIDS, some did not. One of the most vocal doubters has been Peter H. Duesberg, professor of molecular and cell biology at the University of California, Berkeley, who began questioning the HIV theory in 1987. In this 1994 article, Duesberg describes his reasons for thinking that HIV is a harmless passenger virus and that AIDS is actually caused by drugs and other lifestyle factors. Duesberg has explained his ideas at greater length in several books, including *Inventing the AIDS Virus*.

After more than a decade, the war on AIDS has been a dismal failure. At the 1993 International AIDS Conference in Berlin, even the most dogged researchers were beginning to admit their frustration and the mood of the conference was generally pessimistic.

As the number of AIDS victims continues to rise, so do the bewildering questions. Why do so many people infected with the virus remain healthy? Why do homosexuals manifest radically different diseases than the hemophiliacs to whom they donated infected blood? Why can we not, as the most technologically sophisticated biomedical establishment in history, produce a vaccine, as was previously accomplished for polio, measles and other viruses? Where is a safe, effective treatment for AIDS?

Such questions are asked not only by the so-called HIV-AIDS dissidents, such as myself, but also by an increasing number of mainstream AIDS researchers and concerned scientists including the 1994 Nobel laureate in chemistry, Kary Mullis.

A Doubtful Hypothesis

In the early 1990s the U.S. government was spending $6 billion annually for AIDS research and treatment, according to the U.S. Public Health Service. Yet despite spending more than $22 billion since 1982, and despite a staggering 75,000 scientific papers written during the 1980s, a cure for AIDS remains as elusive as ever. It now appears likely that AIDS researchers have made a terrible mistake in blaming HIV, the so-called AIDS virus, for causing AIDS.

This fatal assumption mostly was the result of a rush to judgment in 1984 when virologist Robert Gallo from the National Institutes of Health, along with the Department of Health and Human Services, announced at an international press conference that acquired immune deficiency syndrome was caused by a retrovirus, now known as human immunodeficiency virus.

The announcement was made in the *New York Times* before even one American study on HIV had appeared in scientific literature. It was welcomed by the Reagan administration as a quick answer to gay pressures for a solution to the growing AIDS epidemic. Gallo and his collaborators cited antibodies against the virus in "about 85 percent of patients with AIDS" as the evidence for their hypothesis. Yet that was their only evidence.

Why do so many people infected with the virus remain healthy?

In the scientific papers that followed, HIV was said to cause AIDS by depleting the white blood cells known as T cells. The hypothesis proposed that HIV would cause 30 previously known diseases, including a number of diseases that are not consequences of immunodeficiency, such as cancer, weight loss and dementia.

It now appears that the HIV-AIDS hypothesis is the only link that holds together the 30 heterogenous AIDS diseases. AIDS is defined as a syndrome that occurs only in the presence of HIV. For example, if tuberculosis occurs in the presence of antibodies to HIV, it is AIDS. In the absence of those antibodies, it is tuberculosis. Given this definition, the link between HIV and AIDS is unfalsifiable.

However, to date, the HIV-AIDS hypothesis remains just that—an unproven hypothesis. It is supported only by circumstantial evidence, primarily by the claim that all AIDS patients carry antibodies against HIV. But this correlation is biased by the practice of excluding from AIDS statistics those patients with AIDS-defining diseases in whom no trace of HIV can be found. The disease of such a patient will be diagnosed either by its old name, for example, pneumonia or Kaposi's sarcoma, or will be called idiopathic CD4 lymphocytopenia. This explains why some researchers see the "perfect" correlations between HIV and AIDS.

To date the virus-AIDS hypothesis has failed to yield any public health benefits. No vaccine has been developed and AIDS continues to spread despite efforts to stop the spread of HIV. However, the acid test of a hypothesis is not to produce useful results, but to make accurate predictions.

Unfulfilled Predictions

The HIV-AIDS hypothesis makes the following testable predictions, none of which has been proved.

• AIDS in America would "explode" from the original risk groups via sexual transmission into the general population. Like all other sexually transmitted diseases, AIDS would tend to strike an equal share of both genders.

In America, AIDS has remained in the original risk groups—male homosexuals, male and female intravenous drug users and recipients of transfusions. Since 1981, 90 percent of all American AIDS patients have been males.

• The spread of AIDS would follow the dissemination of HIV.

Although AIDS increased in America from a few hundred to about 50,000 cases annually between 1983 and 1993, HIV did not spread at all. Ever since HIV became detectable in 1985, an unchanging 1 million Americans have been HIV-positive. To account for this discrepancy, defenders of the hypothesis claim the virus has a latency period of 10 years or more.

• Health care workers would contract AIDS from their

patients, scientists from propagating virus and prostitutes from their clients, particularly in the absence of an anti-HIV vaccine or drug.

Not a single confirmed case exists in scientific literature of a health care worker who contracted AIDS from one of the more than 250,000 American AIDS patients. None of the tens of thousands of HIV researchers has developed AIDS from propagating HIV. And prostitutes have not picked up AIDS from their clients—despite the absence of antiviral vaccines or effective drugs.

• Chimpanzees inoculated with HIV would develop AIDS, and the 15,000 American hemophiliacs who were infected iatrogenically [through medical treatments] before 1984 would die from AIDS.

Not one of the 150 chimpanzees inoculated with HIV since 1983 has developed AIDS. Contrary to the prediction, the median life of American hemophiliacs has doubled during the 1980s and early 1990s after 75 percent (15,000) already had been infected by transfusions.

• Natural or vaccine-induced anti-HIV immunity would cure AIDS or protect against future AIDS.

Natural antiviral immunity that is observed in many AIDS patients does not protect against AIDS.

• It would be demonstrated that HIV causes AIDS by killing the white blood cells known as T cells.

The hallmark of all retroviruses is that they do not kill cells that they infect. HIV is the only retrovirus that is asserted to kill its host cell. Several researchers, including HIV discoverer Luc Montagnier, have found that HIV does not kill its host cell in laboratory tests.

• All AIDS diseases are the consequence of HIV-mediated T cell deficiency.

"AIDS does not have the characteristics of an ordinary infectious disease."

About 61 percent of all American AIDS diseases—opportunistic infections such as *Pneumocystis carinii*, candida, tuberculosis etc.—are related to breakdown of the immune system. But 39 percent, including Kaposi's sarcoma, lymphoma, 10 percent weight loss and dementia, are neither caused by nor consistently associated with immunodeficiency. Two studies of homosexuals with Kaposi's sarcoma report that the immune systems of 20 and 19 of the subjects were normal when their disease was first diagnosed.

- AIDS would be restricted by controlling the spread of HIV via "safe sex" and through programs adopting the use of "clean needles" for the injection of street drugs.

AIDS continues to increase despite the safe sex and clean needle programs.

HIV Is Harmless

These points, among many others, give me reason to believe that HIV is in fact a harmless virus. AIDS may be a noninfectious condition "acquired" by recreational drugs and other noncontagious risk factors.

Even proponents of the HIV-AIDS hypothesis, such as Jaap Goudsmit of the University of Amsterdam, have been forced to admit that "AIDS does not have the characteristics of an ordinary infectious disease." Indeed, AIDS does not meet even one of the common criteria of known infectious diseases.

First, all infectious diseases are equally distributed between the genders and never remain tightly segregated in special risk groups. This is especially true of the venereal diseases, including herpes, syphilis, gonorrhea and chlamydia. This also is true of hepatitis [B], the blood-borne virus long considered the model for predicting the spread of HIV. Despite loud publicity to the contrary by vested interests, AIDS has not been spreading to females as predicted nor to the heterosexual population at large.

Second, in all infectious diseases caused by viruses, the virus infects every individual with the disease and the virus is abundant and very active in target tissues during the course of the illness. However, at least 4,621 AIDS cases have been documented since 1984 in which there is no HIV. About one-third of these, 1,691, were recorded in the U.S.; 475 were recorded in Europe and 2,555 in Africa. Since Africa uses only the clinical, rather than the HIV-based AIDS definition, most of these cases were observed there.

Several scientific teams have also documented that, even in those patients who are HIV-infected, the virus is usually totally dormant once immune deficiency is acquired and AIDS appears. Using standard laboratory techniques now available for decades, the active, infectious form of the virus cannot be isolated from the blood or other tissues of most HIV-positive AIDS patients. Even the dormant form of HIV, resting quietly inside infected cells, can be found in only one out of every 1,000 T cells in the patient.

Nor is there a correlation between AIDS and the number of HIV-infected cells. There are, for example, healthy infected individuals with up to 43 times the rate of HIV-infected cells in AIDS patients.

Third, infectious diseases typically follow within days or weeks after infection by viruses, before the immune system has had time to make antibodies against the invader. This is because all viruses begin replicating in the body within hours after infection and multiply into armies of viruses within days or weeks unless stopped by an antiviral immunity. As a rule, viruses strike quickly or not at all. Although it has become fashionable among many scientists to believe in special "slow viruses," or lentiviruses, which are said to take months or years to multiply, such viruses have never actually been found.

In those HIV-positive people who eventually develop AIDS, the syndrome appears only after unpredictable "latent periods" averaging about 10 years. When HIV first infects a person, it can reach moderately high concentrations in the blood—yet AIDS never shows up at that time and T cell levels remain normal. Within days or weeks, the immune system makes antibodies against HIV, and the virus quickly disappears from the blood. Years later, if AIDS shows up at all, the virus rarely comes back to life and multiplies again.

In other words, AIDS never strikes a patient until years after the active virus has been permanently eliminated from the body. This strongly suggests that AIDS is caused by something else.

Drugs Cause AIDS

As an alternative to the HIV explanation, I suggest that AIDS in America and Europe is caused by the long-term use of recreational drugs and by the toxic effects of anti-HIV treatments and that African AIDS is an unrelated epidemic caused by malnutrition, parasitic infections and poor sanitation.

Indeed, AIDS in America and Europe fits all classical criteria of a drug-induced disease syndrome. Part of the evidence for this hypothesis is that about 30 percent of all American and European AIDS patients are intravenous drug users. This group includes nearly all heterosexuals with AIDS. It also includes 80 percent of American and European babies with AIDS who were drug users before birth because their mothers injected drugs during pregnancy.

Since 1982, virtually 10 percent of homosexual males with AIDS or at risk for AIDS have been long-term users of oral, aphrodisiac drugs, particularly nitrite inhalants that confer euphoria and facilitate anal intercourse. Epidemiological studies from San Francisco and Vancouver, British Columbia, have just confirmed, in 1993, that 100 percent of several hundred male homosexuals with AIDS had used multiple recreational drugs. The immunotoxicity of recreational drugs has been documented in the literature since 1909.

It is high time to look at alternative hypotheses of causation.

In addition, some had also used the drug azidothymidine, or AZT, as an antiviral agent. AZT was originally developed 30 years ago to kill human cells in chemotherapy. About 200,000 HIV-positive healthy people and AIDS patients are currently treated four times daily with AZT and other drugs that attack the DNA chains within the cell. But these drugs kill all growing cells, particularly those of the highly proliferative immune system. Thus AZT could, by itself, trigger AIDS. Indeed, Sigma, an American chemical company, accords AZT the highest warning against toxicity, a skull with crossbones.

In the United States, recreational drug use has increased during the 1980s at about the same rate as AIDS. For example, cocaine consumption increased 200-fold from 1980 to 1990, based on the fact that the amount of cocaine seized by authorities increased from 500 kilograms in 1980 to 100,000 kilograms in 1990. During the same period, cocaine-related hospital emergencies increased 24-fold from 3,296 cases in 1981 to 80,355 cases in 1990. Note the increase in AIDS and the rise in cocaine and cocaine-related hospital emergencies run parallel since 1981, whereas HIV has failed to spread since at least 1984.

This would also explain why 90 percent of American

AIDS patients are males, since, according to the Bureau of Justice Statistics, males consume about 75 percent of all illicit injected drugs. In addition, homosexual males are virtually the only consistent users of aphrodisiac drugs such as alkyl nitrites.

Furthermore, we could then explain why AIDS occurs, on average, 10 years after initiation of risk behavior. The great variations in "latent periods" from HIV to AIDS may in fact be the time periods required by individuals to accumulate sufficient drug toxicity to generate AIDS diseases. It takes years of recreational drug consumption to cause disease, just as it frequently takes 20 years of smoking to get lung cancer or emphysema.

In view of the multiple failures of the HIV hypothesis, it is high time to look at alternative hypotheses of causation. But since 1984, virtually every dollar of funding from the federal government for AIDS research has been devoted to work premised on the causal role of HIV and awarded only to grant recipients who do not question that causal role. Such a disproportionate research focus on a single avenue of investigation could conceivably be justified if it had resulted in meaningful advances. Yet, sadly, this massive, narrowly targeted expenditure of public money has not resulted in saving or prolonging a single life.

HIV Causes AIDS

Office of Communications and Public Liaison,
National Institute of Allergy and Infectious Diseases

In this 1994 fact sheet, the National Institute of Allergy and Infectious Diseases (NIAID), part of the National Institutes of Health (an agency of the U.S. Department of Health and Human Services), lists and replies to the objections of Peter Duesberg and others who claim that the virus called HIV does not cause AIDS. NIAID calls these critics' objections "myths" and offers extensive evidence to refute them and support the idea that HIV does cause AIDS.

Myth: HIV antibody testing is unreliable.

Fact: Diagnosis of infection using antibody testing is one of the best-established concepts in medicine. HIV antibody tests exceed the performance of most other infectious disease tests in both sensitivity (the ability of the screening test to give a positive finding when the person tested truly has the disease) and specificity (the ability of the test to give a negative finding when the subjects tested are free of the disease under study). Current HIV antibody tests have sensitivity and specificity in excess of 98% and are therefore extremely reliable.

Progress in testing methodology has also enabled detection of viral genetic material, antigens and the virus itself in body fluids and cells. While not widely used for routine testing due to high cost and requirements in laboratory equipment, these direct testing techniques have confirmed the validity of the antibody tests.

Excerpted from "The Evidence That HIV Causes AIDS," www.niaid.nih.gov, Office of Communications and Public Liaison, National Institute of Allergy and Infectious Diseases, November 29, 2000.

A New Name for Old Diseases?

Myth: There is no AIDS in Africa. AIDS is nothing more than a new name for old diseases.

Fact: The diseases that have come to be associated with AIDS in Africa—such as wasting syndrome, diarrheal diseases and TB—have long been severe burdens there. However, high rates of mortality from these diseases, formerly confined to the elderly and malnourished, are now common among HIV-infected young and middle-aged people, including well-educated members of the middle class. For example, in a study in Cote d'lvoire, HIV-seropositive individuals with pulmonary tuberculosis (TB) were 17 times more likely to die within six months than HIV-seronegative individuals with pulmonary TB. In Malawi, mortality over three years among children who had received recommended childhood immunizations and who survived the first year of life was 9.5 times higher among HIV-seropositive children than among HIV-seronegative children. The leading causes of death were wasting and respiratory conditions. Elsewhere in Africa, findings are similar.

Myth: HIV cannot be the cause of AIDS because researchers are unable to explain precisely how HIV destroys the immune system.

Fact: A great deal is known about the pathogenesis of HIV disease, even though important details remain to be elucidated. However, a complete understanding of the pathogenesis of a disease is not a prerequisite to knowing its cause. Most infectious agents have been associated with the disease they cause long before their pathogenic mechanisms have been discovered. Because research in pathogenesis is difficult when precise animal models are unavailable, the disease-causing mechanisms in many diseases, including tuberculosis and hepatitis B, are poorly understood. The critics' reasoning would lead to the conclusion that *M. tuberculosis* is not the cause of tuberculosis or that hepatitis B virus is not a cause of liver disease.

Myth: AZT and other antiretroviral drugs, not HIV, cause AIDS.

Fact: The vast majority of people with AIDS never received antiretroviral drugs, including those in developed countries prior to the licensure of AZT in 1987, and people in developing countries today where very few individuals have access to these medications.

As with medications for any serious diseases, antiretroviral drugs can have toxic side effects. However, there is no evidence that antiretroviral drugs cause the severe immunosuppression that typifies AIDS, and abundant evidence that antiretroviral therapy, when used according to established guidelines, can improve the length and quality of life of HIV-infected individuals.

A complete understanding of the pathogenesis of a disease is not a prerequisite to knowing its cause.

In the 1980s, clinical trials enrolling patients with AIDS found that AZT given as single-drug therapy conferred a modest (and short-lived) survival advantage compared to placebo. Among HIV-infected patients who had not yet developed AIDS, placebo-controlled trials found that AZT given as single-drug therapy delayed, for a year or two, the onset of AIDS-related illnesses. Significantly, long-term follow-up of these trials did not show a prolonged benefit of AZT, but also never indicated that the drug increased disease progression or mortality. The lack of excess AIDS cases and death in the AZT arms of these placebo-controlled trials effectively counters the argument that AZT causes AIDS.

Subsequent clinical trials found that patients receiving two-drug combinations had up to 50 percent increases in time to progression to AIDS and in survival when compared to people receiving single-drug therapy. In the early 1990s, three-drug combination therapies have produced another 50 percent to 80 percent improvements in progression to AIDS and in survival when compared to two-drug regimens in clinical trials. Use of potent anti-HIV combination therapies has contributed to dramatic reductions in the incidence of AIDS and AIDS-related deaths in populations where these drugs are widely available, an effect which clearly would not be seen if antiretroviral drugs caused AIDS.

Does Behavior Cause AIDS?

Myth: Behavioral factors such as recreational drug use and multiple sexual partners account for AIDS.

Fact: The proposed behavioral causes of AIDS, such as multiple sexual partners and long-term recreational drug use, have existed for many years. The epidemic of AIDS, characterized by the occurrence of formerly rare opportunistic infections such as *Pneumocystis carinii* pneumonia (PCP) did not occur in the United States until a previously unknown human retrovirus—HIV—spread through certain communities.

Compelling evidence against the hypothesis that behavioral factors cause AIDS comes from recent studies that have followed cohorts of homosexual men for long periods of time and found that only HIV-seropositive men develop AIDS.

For example, in a prospectively studied cohort in Vancouver, 715 homosexual men were followed for a median of 8.6 years. Among 365 HIV-positive individuals, 136 developed AIDS. No AIDS-defining illnesses occurred among 350 seronegative men despite the fact that these men reported appreciable use of inhalable nitrites ("poppers") and other recreational drugs, and frequent receptive anal intercourse.

Other studies show that among homosexual men and injection-drug users, the specific immune deficit that leads to AIDS—a progressive and sustained loss of CD4+ T cells—is extremely rare in the absence of other immunosuppressive conditions. For example, in the Multicenter AIDS Cohort Study, more than 22,000 T-cell determinations in 2,713 HIV-seronegative homosexual men revealed only one individual with a CD4+ T-cell count persistently lower than 300 cells/mm^3 of blood, and this individual was receiving immunosuppressive therapy.

In a survey of 229 HIV-seronegative injection-drug users in New York City, mean CD4+ T-cell counts of the group were consistently more than 1000 cells/mm^3 of blood. Only two individuals had two CD4+ T-cell measurements of less than 300/mm^3 of blood, one of whom died with cardiac [heart] disease and non-Hodgkin's lymphoma [a blood cell cancer] listed as the cause of death.

AIDS and Hemophilia

Myth: AIDS among transfusion recipients is due to underlying diseases that necessitated the transfusion, rather than to HIV.

Fact: This notion is contradicted by a report by the Transfusion Safety Study Group (TSSG), which compared HIV-negative and HIV-positive blood recipients who had been given transfusions for similar diseases. Approximately 3 years after the transfusion, the mean CD4+ T-cell count in 64 HIV-negative recipients was 850/mm^3 of blood, while 111 HIV-seropositive individuals had average CD4+ T-cell counts of 375/mm^3 of blood. By 1993, there were 37 cases of AIDS in the HIV-infected group, but not a single AIDS-defining illness in the HIV-seronegative transfusion recipients.

Myth: High usage of clotting factor concentrate, not HIV, leads to CD4+ T-cell depletion and AIDS in hemophiliacs.

Fact: This view is contradicted by many studies. For example, among HIV-seronegative patients with hemophilia A enrolled in the Transfusion Safety Study, no significant differences in CD4+ T-cell counts were noted between 79 patients with no or minimal factor treatment and 52 with the largest amount of lifetime treatments. Patients in both groups had CD4+ T-cell counts within the normal range. In another report from the Transfusion Safety Study, no instances of AIDS-defining illnesses were seen among 402 HIV-seronegative hemophiliacs who had received factor therapy.

In a cohort in the United Kingdom, researchers matched 17 HIV-seropositive hemophiliacs with 17 HIV-seronegative hemophiliacs with regard to clotting factor concentrate usage over a ten-year period. During this time, 16 AIDS-defining clinical events occurred in 9 patients, all of whom were HIV-seropositive. No AIDS-defining illnesses occurred among the HIV-negative patients. In each pair, the mean CD4+ T cell count during follow-up was, on average, 500 cells/mm^3 lower in the HIV-seropositive patient.

Among HIV-infected hemophiliacs, Transfusion Safety Study investigators found that neither the purity nor the amount of Factor VIII therapy had a deleterious effect on CD4+ T cell counts. Similarly, the Multicenter Hemophilia Cohort Study found no association between the cumulative dose of plasma concentrate and incidence of AIDS among HIV-infected hemophiliacs.

Why Do Some People Stay Healthy?

Myth: The distribution of AIDS cases casts doubt on HIV as the cause. Viruses are not gender-specific, yet only a small proportion of AIDS cases are among women.

Fact: The distribution of AIDS cases, whether in the United States or elsewhere in the world, invariably mirrors the prevalence of HIV in a population. In the United States, HIV first appeared in populations of homosexual men and injection-drug users, a majority of whom are male. Because HIV is spread primarily through sex or by the exchange of HIV-contaminated needles during injection-drug use, it is not surprising that a majority of U.S. AIDS cases have occurred in men.

Increasingly, however, women in the United States are becoming HIV-infected usually through the exchange of HIV-contaminated needles or sex with an HIV-infected male. The CDC estimates that 30 percent of new HIV infections in the United States in 1998 were in women. As the number of HIV-infected women has risen, so too has the number of female AIDS patients in the United States. Approximately 23 percent of U.S. adult/adolescent AIDS cases reported to the CDC in 1998 were among women. In 1998, AIDS was the fifth leading cause of death among women aged 25 to 44 in the United States, and the third leading cause of death among African-American women in that age group.

In Africa, HIV was first recognized in sexually active heterosexuals, and AIDS cases in Africa have occurred at least as frequently in women as in men. Overall, the worldwide distribution of HIV infection and AIDS between men and women is approximately 1 to 1.

Compelling evidence against the hypothesis that behavioral factors cause AIDS comes from recent studies.

Myth: HIV cannot be the cause of AIDS because the body develops a vigorous antibody response to the virus.

Fact: This reasoning ignores numerous examples of viruses other than HIV that can be pathogenic after evidence of immunity appears. Measles virus may persist for years in brain cells, eventually causing a chronic neurologic disease despite the presence of antibodies. Viruses such as cytomegalovirus, herpes simplex and varicella zoster may be activated after years of latency even in the presence of abundant antibodies. In animals, viral relatives of HIV with long and variable latency periods, such as visna virus in sheep, cause central nervous system damage even after the production of antibodies.

Also, HIV is well recognized as being able to mutate to avoid the ongoing immune response of the host.

Myth: Only a small number of CD4+ T cells are infected by HIV, not enough to damage the immune system.

Fact: New techniques such as the polymerase chain reaction (PCR) have enabled scientists to demonstrate that a much larger proportion of CD4+ T cells are infected than previously realized, particularly in lymphoid tissues. Macrophages and other cell types are also infected with HIV and serve as reservoirs for the virus. Although the fraction of CD4+ T cells that is infected with HIV at any given time is never extremely high (only a small subset of activated cells serve as ideal targets of infection), several groups have shown that rapid cycles of death of infected cells and infection of new target cells occur throughout the course of disease.

Increasingly . . . women in the United States are becoming HIV-infected.

Myth: HIV is not the cause of AIDS because many individuals with HIV have not developed AIDS.

Fact: HIV disease has a prolonged and variable course. The median period of time between infection with HIV and the onset of clinically apparent disease is approximately 10 years in industrialized countries, according to prospective studies of homosexual men in which dates of seroconversion are known. Similar estimates of asymptomatic periods [periods during which no sign of disease can be seen] have been made for HIV-infected blood-transfusion recipients, injection-drug users and adult hemophiliacs.

As with many diseases, a number of factors can influence the course of HIV disease. Factors such as age or genetic differences between individuals, the level of virulence [ability to cause disease] of the individual strain of virus, as well as exogenous [outside] influences such as co-infection with other microbes may determine the rate and severity of HIV disease expression. Similarly, some people infected with hepatitis B, for example, show no symptoms or only jaundice [yellow skin] and clear their infection, while others suffer disease ranging from chronic liver inflammation to cirrhosis and hepatocellular carcinoma [liver cancer]. Co-factors probably also determine why some smokers develop lung cancer while others do not.

Changeable Illnesses

Myth: Some people have many symptoms associated with AIDS but do not have HIV infection.

Fact: Most AIDS symptoms result from the development of opportunistic infections and cancers associated with severe immunosuppression secondary to HIV.

However, immunosuppression has many other potential causes. Individuals who take glucocorticoids and/or immunosuppressive drugs to prevent transplant rejection or for autoimmune diseases can have increased susceptibility to unusual infections, as do individuals with certain genetic conditions, severe malnutrition and certain kinds of cancers. There is no evidence suggesting that the numbers of such cases have risen, while abundant epidemiologic evidence shows a staggering rise in cases of immunosuppression among individuals who share one characteristic: HIV infection.

Myth: The spectrum of AIDS-related infections seen in different populations proves that AIDS is actually many diseases not caused by HIV.

Fact: The diseases associated with AIDS, such as PCP and *Mycobacterium avium complex* (MAC), are not caused by HIV but rather result from the immunosuppression caused by HIV disease. As the immune system of an HIV-infected individual weakens, he or she becomes susceptible to the particular viral, fungal and bacterial infections common in the community. For example, HIV-infected people in certain midwestern and mid-Atlantic regions are much more likely than people in New York City to develop histoplasmosis, which is caused by a fungus. A person in Africa is exposed to different pathogens than is an individual in an American city. Children may be exposed to different infectious agents than adults.

AZT Offered Hope

Deborah M. Barnes

Deborah M. Barnes, a regular newswriter for *Science* during the 1980s, describes how a large human trial of the drug AZT (azidothymidine) was halted ahead of schedule in September 1986. During the trial, following standard testing procedure, some people with AIDS had received the new drug while others were given a placebo, or inert "dummy pill"; neither the patients nor their doctors knew which treatment a given person was receiving. When patients receiving the placebo showed almost twice as many serious infections and other problems as those receiving AZT, the trial was halted on humanitarian grounds so that everyone could be given the new drug. The U.S. Food and Drug Administration approved AZT in March 1987, making it the first drug to be marketed specifically as a treatment against AIDS.

Officials from the Public Health Service (PHS) and the Burroughs Wellcome Company have announced that AZT, an AIDS drug tested in clinical trials, prolongs the survival of some AIDS patients. The company has terminated its clinical trials prematurely and will make AZT available to additional AIDS patients who meet certain clinical criteria.

"AZT (3-azido-3-deoxythymidine) is not a cure for AIDS," said Robert Windom, assistant secretary for health, who spoke at a news conference announcing the recent decision. "Although the study results we are announcing today hold great promise for prolonging life for certain patients with AIDS, uncertainties remain: uncertainties about possible toxic effects, uncertainties about long-term benefits, or ill effects."

Windom also indicated that he will help facilitate the process by which AZT is approved for commercial distribution. (Burroughs Wellcome will supply AZT free of charge to qualifying patients until the drug is available for sale. The patient's physician must be licensed to practice medicine in the United States and apply for the drug on behalf of an AIDS patient. The PHS and Burroughs Wellcome have established a toll-free information line [1-800-843-9388], open every day from 8 a.m. to midnight, for AIDS patients and their physicians.) First, Burroughs Wellcome must file an application for a new drug. Then, Harry Meyer of the Food and Drug Administration will oversee the approval process, which may be completed by January 1987. After the drug is commercially available, physicians will be able to dispense it by prescription. As a result, clinical trials from 1987 forward will probably include AZT alone or in combination with other drugs.

Startling Results

The impetus for the September 1986 decision came from an independent data safety monitoring board (DSMB), which reviewed preliminary data from clinical trials that were designed to test the effectiveness of AZT in a carefully defined group of patients. Burroughs Wellcome enrolled "only AIDS patients who were within 4 months of their first episode of *Pneumocystis carinii* pneumonia," according to Dannie King of Burroughs Wellcome. "Patients with AIDS-related complex (ARC) and significant disease progression such as weight loss, thrush, fever, and herpes zoster, were also eligible for treatment on this protocol." Because of significantly lower death rates in patients receiving AZT, the DSMB concluded that it would be unethical to continue to withhold the drug from patients participating in the trial who were receiving an inactive placebo compound instead of the drug.

A total of 282 patients participated in the AZT clinical trials at 12 different testing centers in the United States. Only one patient died out of the 145 receiving AZT, but 16 of the 137 patients in the placebo group died—11 with AIDS, and five with ARC. The first patient entered the trial in February 1986 and the last patient was enrolled at the end of June. The trial was originally designed to last until December 1986 and premature termination admittedly compromises its full research value.

In addition to decreasing the mortality rate of AIDS patients with pneumocystis pneumonia, at least over the short term, AZT also seems to improve their quality of life. To varying degrees, AZT recipients had fewer serious medical complications, showed an increase in the number of circulating T4 lymphocytes, could respond to a mild immune stimulus in a skin test, and had an improved sense of well-being.

It would be unethical to continue to withhold the drug.

One of the advantages of AZT is that it crosses the blood-brain barrier and can enter the brain and spinal cord. This property is likely to be of increasing importance as researchers continue to review clinical data, because as many as 60% of AIDS patients have neurological symptoms. These range from mild confusion to global dementia and can also include an impaired ability to move. According to Margaret Fischl of the University of Miami, AZT seems to improve the neurological symptoms of a small number of AIDS patients, but it is still too early to draw conclusions about its full effect on nervous system disease.

To date, the most serious toxic effect of AZT is that it inhibits the normal production of blood cells by the bone marrow. Forty patients who received AZT required transfusions for their anemia, compared to 11 patients from the placebo group who needed transfusions. Another common side effect of AZT was headache.

In addition to giving AZT to all of the AIDS patients participating in the Burroughs Wellcome clinical trial, the drug will also be made available to a much larger number of AIDS patients who meet certain clinical criteria. "The minimum criteria for treatment with AZT will be that AIDS patients have *Pneumocystis carinii* pneumonia, or PCP," according to David Barry of Burroughs Wellcome. PCP is the most common opportunistic infection in AIDS patients and about 60%, or over 6000 people, have the lung infection and may be eligible for AZT. AIDS patients with PCP usually live about 30 to 40 weeks, a time that seems to be extended by treatment with AZT.

Evaluating a Test

The clinical trials concluded in September 1986 comprised the second phase of testing for AZT. The first phase, conducted by the National Cancer Institute (NCI), Duke University, and Burroughs Wellcome, lasted for only 6 weeks. It was designed to determine the safety of the drug in humans and at what dose level it became toxic. Nineteen patients participated in the early tests, 16 of whom were still living in fall 1986, according to Samuel Broder of NCI.

On 20 September, National Institute of Allergy and Infectious Diseases (NIAID) officials met with the principal investigators of 14 newly established treatment evaluation units "to discuss the impact of the AZT results on the design and implementation of future drug trials," said Anthony Fauci, director of NIAID. The units were funded in July 1986 and will test other drugs for AIDS, including dideoxycytidine, ribavirin, HPA-23, foscarnet, and interferon alpha. Fauci says that future clinical trials are likely to include tests of AZT alone or in combination with another drug.

On 24 September, NIH and Burroughs Wellcome officials decided on a more detailed description of the clinical criteria that AIDS patients must meet in order to receive AZT. The best candidates for future clinical trials may be patients that have not developed serious infections or illness. These include persons infected with the AIDS virus who show no symptoms of the disease, patients with early Kaposi's sarcoma affecting only the skin, and patients with chronically swollen lymph nodes. Fauci thinks that even after AZT becomes commercially available, "there will be people who are cautious enough about AZT and its side effects to participate in placebo-controlled clinical trials."

It is still too early to pinpoint exactly how and why AZT has decreased . . . mortality.

The data safety monitoring board that recommended the premature termination of the AZT trial is a six-member panel composed of clinicians, a biostatistician, and a bioethicist. None are employed by Burroughs Wellcome nor were any of the board's members involved in the clinical trials. The board met on 1 August, 10 September, and 18 September 1986 to evaluate preliminary clinical data from the AZT trial.

Even though the study reviewed by the board included ARC patients, "the termination of the study was based upon the results that were seen in a particular group of AIDS patients, those who recently had developed PCP," said Fauci. "But the story isn't over with AZT. AZT will be studied further in other groups and the data that have already been collected will be analyzed in more detail. We expect to learn more about AZT and its effect on a variety of other components of AIDS."

Mysterious but Effective

In fact, it is still too early to pinpoint exactly how and why AZT has decreased the mortality rate in patients with AIDS and pneumocystis pneumonia. The drug blocks the ability of the AIDS virus to replicate inside a host cell. It interrupts elongation of chains of DNA, making it impossible for the virus to complete DNA synthesis and thus reproduce itself. But how these molecular events, which were initially deduced by studying the action of AZT on virus-infected cells growing in laboratory culture dishes, translate into the clinical improvement of AIDS patients is still not clear.

"Scientifically, understanding how this drug works in AIDS patients could be one of the most exciting things right now," says Fauci. One clear effect the AZT seems to have in people is that it allows the immune system to restore itself partially, at least for a while. "We know that the number of T4 lymphocytes in patients receiving AZT increases, peaks, and then comes down, but the patients continue to do well," according to Fauci. Presumably, the time-delayed fall in the number of T4 cells occurs with bone marrow suppression.

But scientists have no direct evidence that AZT blocks viral replication in AIDS patients as it does in cultured cells. "There is no difference in our ability to isolate and grow the AIDS virus from patients who receive AZT," says Fauci. Fauci thinks that AZT may block the active replication of the virus in human cells, but that it may not affect virus that has inserted itself into the DNA of a host cell to remain there, perhaps for very long periods of time, in a dormant state.

The AIDS virus is spread by sexual contact with an infected person, by the exchange of blood during intravenous drug use, in contaminated blood or blood products, or from an infected mother to her infant during pregnancy or childbirth. As of 15 September 1986, there were 24,859 reported cases of AIDS in the United States, and 11,170 patients are still alive. An estimated 1.5 to 2 million people are infected with the virus.

All of the health officials, as well as the representatives from Burroughs Wellcome stress that it is still too early to tell how effective AZT will be as a long-term therapy in AIDS. Only a few patients have received the drug for a year, and most have received it for 6 months or less. Thus, the potential effectiveness of AZT, as well as its potential toxicity, are simply unknown over the long term. It remains, however, the only therapy for AIDS that has shown even partial effectiveness.

7

AZT Was a Failure

Celia Farber

AZT, the first drug that the U.S. Food and Drug Administration approved for the treatment of AIDS, was widely hailed by people with AIDS and their physicians in the late 1980s. However, Celia Farber argues in this investigative article that AZT is a highly toxic substance, likely to do more harm than good. She claims that it was approved on the basis of inadequate testing because of political pressure to develop a treatment—any treatment—for the deadly disease. Farber, who at the time of this article was a senior editor of *Spin* and author of a regular column on AIDS, is especially critical of the idea of giving AZT to HIV-positive people who show no signs of AIDS, let alone healthy people considered at high risk for the disease, such as health care workers who treat people with AIDS. The drug, she maintains, will destroy such people's immune systems more surely than the disease itself. Farber has written about HIV and AIDS for more than a decade and is a regular contributor to *Spin*, *Esquire*, *Gear*, and *USA Today*.

On a cold January day in 1987, inside one of the brightly-lit meeting rooms of the monstrous Food and Drug Administration (FDA) building, a panel of 11 top AIDS doctors pondered a very difficult decision. They had been asked by the FDA to consider giving lightning-quick approval to a highly toxic drug about which there was very little information. Clinically called Zidovudine, but nicknamed AZT after its components, the drug was said to have shown a dramatic effect on the survival of AIDS patients. The study that had brought the panel together had set the medical community

Excerpted from "Sins of Omission," by Celia Farber, *Spin*, November 1989.

abuzz. It was the first flicker of hope—people were dying much faster on the placebo than on the drug.

But there were tremendous concerns about the new drug. It had actually been developed a quarter of a century earlier as a cancer chemotherapy, but was shelved and forgotten because it was so toxic, very expensive to produce, and totally ineffective against cancer. Powerful, but unspecific, the drug was not selective in its cell destruction.

AZT, which several members of the panel still . . . feared could be a time bomb, was approved.

Drug companies around the world were sifting through hundreds of compounds in the race to find a cure, or at least a treatment, for AIDS. Burroughs Wellcome, a subsidiary of Wellcome, a British drug company, emerged as the winner. By chance, they sent the failed cancer drug, then known as Compound S, to the National Cancer Institute along with many others to see if it could slay the AIDS dragon, HIV. In the test tube at least, it did.

At the meeting, there was a lot of uncertainty and discomfort with AZT. The doctors who had been consulted knew that the study was flawed and that the long-range effects were completely unknown. But the public was almost literally baying at the door. Understandably, there was immense pressure on the FDA to approve AZT quickly.

Hurried Approval

Everybody was worried about this one. To approve it, said Ellen Cooper, an FDA director, would represent a "significant and potentially dangerous departure from our normal toxicology requirements."

Just before approving the drug, one doctor on the panel, Calvin Kunin, summed up their dilemma. "On the one hand," he said, "to deny a drug which decreases mortality in a population such as this would be inappropriate. On the other hand, to use this drug widely, for areas where efficacy has not been demonstrated, with a potentially toxic agent, might be disastrous."

"We do not know what will happen a year from now," said panel chairman Dr. Itzhak Brook. "The data is just too premature, and the statistics are not really well done. The drug could actually be detrimental." A little later, he said he was also "struck by the facts that AZT does not stop deaths. Even those who were switched to AZT still kept dying."

"I agree with you," answered another panel member, "There are so many unknowns. Once a drug is approved there is no telling how it could be abused. There's no going back."

Burroughs Wellcome reassured the panel that they would provide detailed two-year follow-up data, and that they would not let the drug get out of its intended parameters: as a stopgap measure for very sick patients.

Dr. Brook was not won over by the promise. "If we approve it today, there will not be much data. There will be a promise of data," he predicted, "but then the production of data will be hampered." Brook's vote was the only one cast against approval.

The most serious problem with the original study . . . is that it was never completed.

"There was not enough data, not enough follow-up," Brook recalls. "Many of the questions we asked the company were answered by, 'We have not analyzed the data yet,' or 'We do not know.' I felt that there was some promising data, but I was very worried about the price being paid for it. The side effects were so very severe. It was chemotherapy. Patients were going to need blood transfusions. That's very serious.

"The committee was tending to agree with me," says Brook, "that we should wait a little bit, be more cautious. But once the FDA realized we were intending to reject it, they applied political pressure. At about 4 p.m., the head of the FDA's Center for Drugs and Biologics asked permission to speak, which is extremely unusual. Usually they leave us alone. But he said to us, 'Look, if you approve the drug, we can assure you that we will work together with Burroughs Wellcome and make sure the drug is given to the right people.' It was like saying 'please do it.'"

Brad Stone, FDA press officer, was at that meeting. He says he doesn't recall that particular speech, but that there is nothing "unusual" about FDA officials making such speeches at advisory meetings. "The people in that meeting approved the drug because the data the company had produced proved it was prolonging life. Sure it was toxic, but they concluded that the benefits clearly outweighed the risks."

The meeting ended. AZT, which several members of the panel still felt uncomfortable with and feared could be a time bomb, was approved.

An Invalid Study

Flash forward: August 17, 1989. Newspapers across America banner-headlined that AZT had been "proven to be effective in HIV antibody-positive, asymptomatic and early ARC patients," even though one of the panel's main concerns was that the drug should only be used in a last-case scenario for critically-ill AIDS patients, due to the drug's extreme toxicity. Dr. Anthony Fauci, head of the National Institutes of Health (NIH), was now pushing to expand prescription.

The FDA's traditional concern had been thrown to the wind. Already the drug had spread to 60 countries and an estimated 20,000 people. Not only had no new evidence allayed the initial concerns of the panel, but the follow-up data, as Dr. Brook predicted, had fallen by the wayside. The beneficial effects of the drug had been proven to be temporary. The toxicity, however stayed the same.

The majority of those in the AIDS afflicted and medical communities held the drug up as the first breakthrough on AIDS. For better or worse, AZT had been approved faster than any drug in FDA history, and activists considered it a victory. The price paid for the victory, however, was that almost all government drug trials, from then on, focused on AZT—while over 100 other promising drugs were left uninvestigated.

Burroughs Wellcome stock went through the roof when the announcement was made. At a price of $8,000 per patient per year (not including blood work and transfusions), AZT is the most expensive drug ever marketed. Burroughs Wellcome's gross profits for 1990 are estimated at $230 million. Stock market analysts predict that Burroughs Wellcome may be selling as much as $2 billion worth of AZT, under the brand name Retrovir, each year by the mid-1990s—matching Burroughs Wellcome's total sales for all its products in 1988.

AZT is the only antiretroviral drug that has received FDA approval for treatment of AIDS since the epidemic began in 1980, and the decision to approve it was based on a single study that has long been declared invalid.

The study was intended to be a "double-blind placebo-controlled study," the only kind of study that can effectively prove whether or not a drug works. In such a study, neither patient nor doctor is supposed to know if the patient is getting the drug or a placebo. In the case of AZT, the study became unblinded on all sides, after just a few weeks.

Both sides of the study contributed to the unblinding. It became obvious to doctors who was getting what because AZT causes such severe side effects that AIDS per se does not. Furthermore, a routine blood count known as CMV, which clearly shows who is on the drug and who is not, wasn't whited out in the reports. Both of these facts were accepted and confirmed by both the FDA and Burroughs Wellcome, who conducted the study.

AZT is effective for a few months, but . . . its effect drops off sharply after that.

Many of the patients who were in the trial admitted that they had analyzed their capsules to find out whether they were getting the drug. If they weren't, some bought the drug on the underground market. Also, the pills were supposed to be indistinguishable by taste, but they were not. Although this was corrected early on, the damage was already done. There were also reports that patients were pooling pills out of solidarity to each other. The study was so severely flawed that its conclusions must be considered, by the most basic scientific standards, unproven.

The most serious problem with the original study, however, is that it was never completed. Seventeen weeks in the study, in September 1986, when more patients had died in the placebo group, the study was stopped short, and all subjects were put on AZT. No scientific study can ever be conducted to prove unequivocally whether AZT does prolong life.

Dr. Brook, who voted against approval, warned at the time that AZT, being the only drug available for doctors to prescribe to AIDS patients, would probably have a runaway effect. Approving it prematurely, he said, would be like "letting the genie out of the bottle."

Brook pointed out that since the drug is a form of chemotherapy, it should only be prescribed by doctors who have experience with chemotherapeutic drugs. Because of the most severe toxic effects of AZT—cell depletion of the bone marrow—patients would need frequent blood transfusions. As if happened, AZT was rampantly prescribed as soon as it was released, way beyond its purported parameters. The worst-case scenario had come true: Doctors interviewed by the *New York Times* later in 1987 revealed that they were already giving AZT to healthy people who had tested positive for antibodies to HIV.

The FDA's function is to weigh a drug's efficacy against its potential hazards. The equation is simple and obvious: A drug must unquestionably repair more than it damages, otherwise the drug itself may cause more harm than the disease it is supposed to fight. Exactly what many doctors and scientists fear is happening with AZT . . . .

Success or Failure?

Several studies on the clinical effects of AZT—including the one that Burroughs Wellcome's approval was based on—have drawn the same conclusion: that AZT is effective for a few months, but that its effect drops off sharply after that. Even the original AZT study showed that T-4 cells went up for a while and then plummeted. HIV levels went down, and then came back up. This fact was well-known when the advisory panel voted for approval. As panel member Dr. Stanley Lemon said in the meeting, "I am left with the nagging thought after seeing several of these slides, that after 16 to 24 weeks—12 to 16 weeks, I guess—the effect seems to be declining."

A follow-up meeting, two years after the original Burroughs Wellcome study, was scheduled to discuss the long range effects of AZT, and the survival statistics. As one doctor present at that meeting in May 1988 recalls "They hadn't followed up the study. Anything that looked beneficial was gone within half a year. All they had were some survival statistics averaging 44 weeks. The p24 didn't pan out and there was no persistent improvement in the T-4 cells."

HIV levels in the blood are measured by an antigen called p24. Burroughs Wellcome made the claim that AZT lowered this level, that is, lowered the amount of HIV in the blood. At the first FDA meeting, Burroughs Wellcome emphasized how the drug had "lowered" the p24 levels; at the follow-up meeting, they didn't mention it.

As that meeting was winding down, Dr. Michael Lange, head of the AIDS program at St. Luke's-Roosevelt Hospital in New York, spoke up about this. "The claim of AZT is made on the fact that it is supposed to have an antiviral effect," he said to Burroughs Wellcome, "and on this we have seen no data at all . . . Since there is a report in the *Lancet* [a leading British medical journal] that after 20 weeks or so, in many patients p24 came back, do you have any data on that?"

They didn't.

"What counts is the bottom line," one of the scientists representing Burroughs Wellcome summed up, "the survival, the neurologic function, the absence of progression and the quality of life, all of which are better. Whether you call it better because of some antiviral effect, or some other antibacterial effect, they are still better."

Dr. Lange suggested that the drug may be effective the same way a simple anti-inflammatory, such as aspirin, is effective. An inexpensive, nontoxic drug called Indomecithin, he pointed out, might serve the same function, without the devastating side effects.

One leading AIDS researcher, who was part of the FDA approval process, says in late 1989: "Does AZT do anything? Yes, it does. But the evidence that it does something against HIV is really not there."

"I wouldn't take AZT if you paid me."

"There have always been drugs that we use without knowing exactly how they work," says Nobel Prize winner Walter Gilbert. "The really important thing to look at is the clinical effect. Is the drug helping or isn't it?"

"I'm living proof that AZT works," says one person with ARC [AIDS-related complex] on AZT. "I've been on it for two years now, and I'm certainly healthier than I was two years ago. It's not a cure-all, it's not a perfect drug, but it is effective. It's slowing down the progression of the disease."

"Sometimes I feel like I'm swallowing Drano," says another. "I mean, sometimes I have problems swallowing. I just don't like the idea of taking something that foreign to my body. But every six hours, I've got to swallow it. Until something better comes along, this is what is available to me."

Rejecting AZT

"I am absolutely convinced that people enjoy a better quality of life and survive longer who do not take AZT," says Gene Fedorko, President of Health Education AIDS Liaison (HEAL). "I think it's horrible the way people are bullied by their doctors to take the drug. We get people coming to us shaking and crying because their doctors said they'll die if they don't take AZT. That is an absolute lie." Fedorko has drawn his conclusion from years of listening to the stories of people struggling to survive AIDS at HEAL's weekly support group.

"I wouldn't take AZT if you paid me," says Michael Callen, cofounder of New York City's coalition of people with AIDS (PWAs), Community Research Initiative, and editor of several AIDS journals. Callen has survived AIDS for over seven years without the help of AZT. "I've gotten the shit kicked out me for saying this, but I think using AZT is like aiming a thermonuclear warhead at a mosquito. The overwhelming majority of long-term survivors I've known have chosen not to take AZT."

The last surviving patient from the original AZT trial, according to Burroughs Wellcome, died in late 1989. When he died, he had been on AZT for three and one-half years. He was the longest surviving AZT recipient. The longest surviving AIDS patient overall, not on AZT, has lived for eight and one-half years.

An informal study of long-term survivors of AIDS followed 24 long-term survivors, all of whom had survived AIDS more than six years. Only one of them had recently begun taking AZT.

In the early days, AZT was said to extend lives. In actual fact, there is simply no solid evidence that AZT prolongs life.

"I think AZT does prolong life in most people," says Dr. Bruce Montgomery of the State University of New York City at Stony Brook, who is completing a study on AZT. "There are not very many long-term survivors, and we really don't know why they survive. It could be luck. But most people are not so lucky."

"AZT does seem to help many patients," says Dr. Bernard Bahari, a New York City AIDS physician and researcher, "but it's very hard to determine whether it actually prolongs life."

"Many of the patients I see choose not to take AZT," says Dr. Don Abrams of San Francisco General Hospital. "I've been impressed that survival and lifespan are increasing for all people with AIDS. I think it has a lot to do with aerosolized Pentamidine [a drug that treats *pneumocystis carinii* pneumonia]. There's also the so-called plague effect, the fact that people get stronger and stronger when a disease hits a population. The patients I see today are not as fragile as the early patients were."

"Whether you live or die with AIDS is a function of how well your doctor treats you, not of AZT," says Dr. Joseph Sonnabend, one of New York's City's first and most reputable AIDS doctors, whose patients include many long-term survivors, although he has never prescribed AZT. Sonnabend was one of the first to make the simple observation that AIDS patients should be treated for their diseases, not just for their HIV infection.

"We're being held hostage by second-rate scientists."

Several studies have concluded that AZT has no effect on the two most common opportunistic AIDS infections, *Pneumocystis carinii* Pneumonia (PCP) and Kaposi's Sarcoma (KS). The overwhelming majority of AIDS patients die of PCP, for which there has been an effective treatment for decades. In 1989, the FDA finally approved aerosolized Pentamidine for AIDS. A 1989 Memorial Sloan Kettering study concluded the following: By 15 months, 80% of people on AZT not receiving Pentamidine had a recurring episode. "All those deaths in the AZT study were treatable," Sonnabend says. "They weren't deaths from AIDS, they were deaths from treatable conditions. They didn't even do autopsies for that study. What kind of faith can one have in these people?"

"If there's any resistance to AZT in the general public at all, it's within the gay community of New York," says the doctor close to the FDA approval, who asked to remain anonymous. "The rest of the country has been brainwashed into thinking this drug really does that much. The data has all been manipulated by people who have a lot vested in AZT."

"If AIDS were not the popular disease that it is—the money-making and career-making machine—these people could not get away with that kind of shoddy science," says Bialy. "In all of my years in science I have never seen anything this atrocious." When asked if he thought it was at all possible that people have been killed as a result of AZT poisoning rather than AIDS he answered: "It's more than possible." . . .

AZT for Well People?

Burroughs Wellcome has already launched testing of AZT in asymptomatic hospital workers, pregnant women, and in children, who are getting liquid AZT. The liquid is left over from an aborted trial, and given to the children because they can mix it with water—children don't like to swallow pills. It has also been proposed that AZT be given to people who do not yet even test positive for HIV antibodies, but are "at risk."

"I'm convinced that if you gave AZT to a perfectly healthy athlete," says Fedorko, "he would be dead in five years."

In December 1988, the *Lancet* published a study that Burroughs Wellcome and the NIH do not include in their press kits. It was more expansive than the original AZT study and followed patients longer. It was not conducted in the United States, but in France, at the Claude Bernard Hospital in Paris, and concluded the same thing about AZT that Burroughs Wellcome's study did, except Burroughs Wellcome called their results "overwhelmingly positive," and the French doctors called theirs "disappointing." The French study found, once again, that AZT was too toxic for most to tolerate, had no lasting effect on HIV blood levels, and left the patients with fewer T-4 cells than they started with. Although they noticed a clinical improvement at first, they concluded that "by six months, these values had returned to their pretreatment levels and several opportunistic infections, malignancies and deaths occurred."

"Thus the benefits of AZT are limited to a few months for ARC and AIDS patients," the French team concluded. After a few months, the study found, AZT was completely ineffective.

The news that AZT will soon be prescribed to asymptomatic people has left many leading AIDS doctors dumbfounded and furious. Every doctor and scientist I asked felt that it was highly unprofessional and reckless to announce a study with no data to look at, making recommendations with such drastic public health implications. "This simply does not happen," says Bialy. "The government is reporting scientific facts before they've been reviewed? It's unheard of."

"It's beyond belief," says Dr. Sonnabend in a voice tinged with desperation. "I don't know what to do. I have to go in and face an office full of patients asking for AZT. I'm terrified. I don't know what to do as a responsible physician. The first study was ridiculous. Margaret Fishl, who has done both of these studies, obviously doesn't know the first thing about clinical trials. I don't trust her. Or the others. They're simply not good enough. We're being held hostage by second-rate scientists. We let them get away with the first disaster; now they're doing it again."

"It's a momentous decision to say to people, 'if you're HIV-positive and your T4-cells are below 500 start taking AZT,'" says the doctor who wished to remain anonymous. "I know dozens of people that I've seen personally every few months for several years now who have been in that state for more than five years, and have not progressed to any disease. I have stopped prescribing AZT because I have consistently found that my patients who don't take it live longer."

"I'm ashamed of my colleagues," Sonnabend laments. "I'm embarrassed. This is such shoddy science it's hard to believe nobody is protesting. Damned cowards. The name of the game is protect your grants, don't open your mouth. It's all about money . . . it's grounds for just following the party line and not being critical, when there are obviously financial and political forces that are driving this."

When Peter Duesberg [a scientist who questions whether HIV causes AIDS] heard the announcement in August 1989, he was particularly stunned over the reaction of Gay Men's Health Crisis (GMHC) President Richard Dunne, who said that GMHC now urged "everybody to get tested," and of course those who test positive to go on AZT. "These people are running into the gas chambers," says Duesberg. "Himmler would have been so happy if only the Jews were this cooperative."

Chapter 2

Society Confronts AIDS

1

Society Views a Mystery Plague

Loudon Wainwright

Loudon Wainwright is a singer, songwriter, and actor. He wrote the following selection in mid-1983, a mere two years after the first medical reports of AIDS were published and before the disease's cause and methods of spreading had been identified. Wainwright points out, but distances himself from, the homophobic quality of the fear that was beginning to spread throughout American society regarding this "gay-related" disease. He identifies with the isolation that the disease's victims feel and admires their courage in dealing with societal rejection as well as a fatal malady. Nonetheless, he admits that he cannot avoid completely the concern that he might somehow contract the illness.

Assured and neat in his dark blue suit, the young man testified before a New York State Senate committee about a new and terrifying disease. "My life has become totally controlled by AIDS and my fight to recover," he said. "I am subject to fevers and night sweats and an unendurable fatigue. I live with the fear that every cold or sore throat or skin rash may be a sign of something more serious. At the age of 28, I wake up every morning to face the very real possibility of my own death."

Michael Callen is one of more than 1,500 people who have been diagnosed between 1981 and 1983 as having Acquired Immune Deficiency Syndrome, a complex disease of unknown origin about which fears of death are appropriate.

Excerpted from "Cries of Plague for Mysterious AIDS," by Loudon Wainwright, *Life*, July 1983.

There is no known treatment for it; only the diseases that come in its wake can be fought directly. According to some calculations, it eventually kills more than 80 percent of its victims, most within two to three years.

Unknown Transmission Creates Fear

Like 70 percent of AIDS victims, Callen is a gay male who has had many sexual partners, which suggests to researchers that the disease is transmitted sexually. But there are other possibilities. The fact that many among the rest of the ill are drug users who use needles or hemophiliacs, who require frequent blood transfusions, suggests that it is transmitted by blood. That five percent of those with AIDS are natives of Haiti with no clear hemophilic, homosexual or drug-use background has almost everybody puzzled. And because a very few patients seem to fit into none of the categories, many people are badly frightened.

Their fear, of course, is that the disease, which has already been called an epidemic by authorities and is cropping up at a rate of three to five new cases a day, will be spread uncontrollably by casual, even unknowing contacts into the general population. The fear, in fact, is quite possibly more dangerous and degrading than the pestilence.

"We remind people of death."

Yet inspite of the terrified, angry and often homophobic quality of some of the cries of plague (one columnist wrote: "The poor homosexuals—they have declared war upon nature, and now nature is exacting an awful retribution"), there is no good evidence that AIDS can be passed along by ordinary contact or taken literally from the air surrounding the victims, the way one picks up a cold. Among those attempting to stave off hysteria is the U.S. Public Health Service's top doctor, Edward N. Brandt Jr., who, reporting recently that AIDS had become the Services "Number One Priority," added that citizens should not be either "unduly frightened or overly complacent" about it. A possible translation of that rather mixed reassurance: This is a big, frightening, mysterious problem. But don't panic.

For people who actually have AIDS, not panicking is a tall order; most of the gay men, for example, are quite young, in their 20s and 30s. Mortality, whose bleak reality is usually held off until much later, has suddenly become the overriding issue of their lives. Early this month I spent an evening with Callen and a group of other AIDS patients in a New York coffee shop. Sitting with them around a big table, I had to remind myself that some were very ill. Most looked relatively healthy to me, and when we began there was some easy joking. But, in fact, several had recently been in hospitals with one or another of the many "opportunistic" infections that commonly hit patients whose immunological defenses are down, and they had all just come from a self-help meeting that 20 to 30 victims attend each week.

"This thing has made me look hard at myself."

"We remind people of death" one of the older men at the table said in response to a question about how people treat them. And more than that, I thought. They remind people of the pain and helplessness that go with an awful illness. "We're thought of as lepers," said another. "And not just by outsiders. Sometimes by our friends and familes, as well." The list of examples that followed covered a lot of sad ground: frightened lovers had fled; a sick man had been asked not to come home for Christmas; another could tell his mother only that he had lymphoma ("As much as everyone hates cancer, they hate AIDS more").

The number of stories about the rejection of people with AIDS is increasing every day. Some are understandable, some are contemptible. Hospital workers occasionally refuse to touch them. Patients come home to find landlords trying to have them kicked out of their apartments. Others face firing because their employers fear contamination on the job. "They're trying to create a new level of contagion," one angry man told me. "Just for us."

I remembered suddenly that when I'd had polio as a child of 12, someone had told me there was a quarantine sign on the door warning people away from the house. At first it had thrilled me—I was a character in some book about the Middle Ages. But then I felt a sense of horror, of my own real apartness. Their brutal casting-out has a predictably demoralizing effect on the AIDS victims. "It feeds into my own paranoia," another man said. "I'm like everybody else—I believe what I read. I have three nieces in Pennsylvania. I adore them. Can I go over there and hug them."

Helping Others, Helping Themselves

Yet from talking with them, I found that a number of individuals and organizations, especially in New York and San Francisco, give AIDS patients a lot of guidance and support. With its hundreds of volunteers in New York, the Gay Men's Health Crisis runs a 24-hour hot line, raises funds for research (the U.S. government has allocated $14.5 million for AIDS study in fiscal 1983), offers counseling for victims trying to deal with the crushing news of their illness. It also provides help at home for those too sick to take care of themselves and has set up free therapy groups for the victims, their parents and their lovers.

At New York University Medical Center I talked with social worker Noreen Russell about the therapy groups that she and a colleague have been conducting for AIDS patients since 1981. Some have been very sick with Kaposi's sarcoma, the rare and usually mild skin cancer that seems to turn fierce with AIDS victims. Of her first group of eight, half have died, and there have been three deaths in her current group too. "If a friend dies of it," Russell said, "they question if they're going to be next."

But time and careful therapy help, and some patients feel well enough to leave the group. "We try to get them to put as much quality as possible into their lives," Russell said. One, she recalled, had seemed close to suicidal when he started in the group, and it appeared at least possible he would not wait for the disease to kill him. "Now," said Russell, "he realizes how much he wants to live."

The men in the coffee shop reported they felt better too. "This thing has made me look hard at myself," one said. "I've changed my diet and am getting a lot of exercise. I'm involved in aggressive caretaking—of me." Another said, "It helped me figure out who was important to me. People I felt close to got closer."

Touched and impressed with their courage, I found myself haunted by their poor possibilities. Is it likely that ways will be found soon to treat the sickness that hides in them and God knows how many others? Will the virulent rejection by some that damns the whole homosexual population along with the ill make the rising alarm about AIDS much worse? I don't know. The fear of contagion is hard to fight. When the group at the coffee shop broke up, I shook hands with several of the men. "Better wash your hands," one said in friendly derision as he left. With a certain shame, I realized I'd been considering it.

America's Response to AIDS Verged on Hysteria

Evan Thomas

Evan Thomas, a reporter for *Time* in the 1980s, wrote the following article for that magazine in 1985. In it he describes the anxiety that swept mainstream America as AIDS was shown to strike a widening circle of individuals, including children and heterosexuals. By that time, Evans points out, scientists had identified the cause of the disease and shown that it could not be spread by casual contact, such as sharing food. Nonetheless, parents were demanding that children with AIDS not be allowed to attend public schools, and people who had—or even were suspected of having—AIDS were being evicted from their apartments. Thomas is now a current events reporter for *Newsweek*. He has also written for publications such as *The New York Times Book Review* and *The Washington Post*.

There were 946,000 children attending New York City schools, and only one of them—an unidentified second-grader enrolled at an undisclosed school—was known to suffer from acquired immunodeficiency syndrome, the dread disease known as AIDS. But the parents of children at P.S. 63 in Queens, one of the city's 622 elementary schools, were not taking any chances in early September 1985. As the school opened its doors for the fall term, 944 of its 1,100 students stayed home.

That evening, hundreds of anxious parents gathered in

From "The New Untouchables," by Evan Thomas, *Time*, September 23, 1985.

the school's airless auditorium. They chanted, "Two, four, six, eight, no AIDS in any grades!" and waved placards proclaiming OUR CHILDREN WANT GOOD GRADES, NOT AIDS! Local politicians stirred the pot. "This is not meant to scare you," City Councilman Joseph Lisa of Queens began, "but leading medical researchers throughout the world truly believe that this epidemic may well be the most serious epidemic in recorded medical history." Chimed in State Assemblyman Frederick Schmidt: "There is no medical authority who can say with authority that AIDS cannot be transmitted in school. What about somebody sneezing in the classroom? What about the water fountain? What about kids who get in a fight with a bloody nose? They don't know!" The crowd screamed and stomped. Cried Schmidt: "We should not experiment with our children!"

Anxiety over AIDS in some parts of the U.S. is verging on hysteria.

Anxiety over AIDS in some parts of the U.S. is verging on hysteria. The boycott that kept home 12,000 of the 47,000 students in two Queens school districts on the first day of school last week was only the most dramatic display of the panic that has made virtual lepers out of many AIDS victims.

No longer is AIDS regarded as a "gay plague" that strikes down only promiscuous male homosexuals or heavy intravenous-drug users. Now children and heterosexuals are seen as vulnerable. The disclosure in July 1985 that actor Rock Hudson suffers from AIDS has made the public more aware and helped generate more funding for AIDS-related research. Yet the publicity seems to have created more fear than understanding in U.S. communities.

• In Miami, a highly successful caterer and floral designer named David Harrison was ruined when word spread that he had AIDS. Old clients, even hospitals, suddenly shunned him.

• In Anaheim, Calif., in September 1985, Episcopal Bishop William E. Swing distributed a pastoral letter to counsel the "cautious person" who fears catching AIDS by drinking wine from a common cup. Eating bread was deemed adequate Communion.

• In San Antonio, County Judge Tony Jimenez arraigned a prisoner tested positive for AIDS in the man's jail cell, lest the courtroom and staff get contaminated.

• In New Orleans, the local AIDS task force gets calls from citizens asking if the disease can be spread by mosquitoes. "If that were true, the whole city of New Orleans would have AIDS," sighs the agency's chairman, Dr. Louise McFarland.

"People are scared—even medical professionals," says Linda Berkowitz, district administrator for the Florida department of health and rehabilitative services. "There are still so many unanswered questions, and myths abound."

The fear is greatly out of proportion to the actual risk. Though the disease is invariably fatal, and the number of AIDS cases (now 13,000) has been doubling every ten months, the heterosexual population has scarcely been touched. The vast majority of AIDS victims (73%) are male homosexuals or bisexuals, and most of the rest are drug abusers. Nonetheless, when asked by a CBS-*New York Times* poll to name "the most serious medical problems facing the country," more people cited AIDS than heart disease, the nation's leading killer (75,961 deaths last year). Experts agree that AIDS can be spread only through intimate sexual conduct, the use of a contaminated hypodermic needle, transfusions of blood containing the virus, or, in the case of a newborn, from an infected mother. But many people remain ignorant or simply doubt the evidence. The CBS-*Times* poll found that 47% think that AIDS can be contracted via a drinking glass, and 28% believe the disease can be picked up from a toilet seat.

"This isn't mass hysteria, it's frightened, unified parents," says Annette Maiorana, a Queens mother who kept her eight-year-old out of school in September 1985. "In school, kids share their milk, they share sandwiches, they spit at each other. There's urine on the toilet seats. They chew on a pencil and give it to a friend. I have a little one ready to go to preschool, and it's frightening."

The Centers for Disease Control in Atlanta advises that most children suffering from AIDS, unless they are handicapped, unable to control body secretions or given to biting other children, should be allowed to attend school. But many local officials wonder if the experts are underestimating the threat. Protests Marvin Aaron, a district superintendent in Queens: "I don't want all the medical experts telling me 'Don't worry.' I'm worrying." His School District No. 27 went to court in mid-September to block the enrollment of the student with AIDS, apparently a girl whose disease is said to be in remission. The case is pending.

Some local schools have already barred AIDS patients from the classroom. Washington Borough in New Jersey turned away a four-year-old girl with AIDS-related complex (ARC) and her nine-year-old brother, even though he is not ill. In Washington, a child with AIDS is tutored alone in a separate room at school, and in Kokomo, Ind., a 13-year-old hemophiliac with the disease has been instructed at home over a phone hookup.

In Swansea, Mass., a boy suffering from AIDS was allowed to attend his eighth-grade class earlier this month, and only half a dozen of the school's 630 students were kept home by parents. But many parents bitterly railed against "the fancy talk" of experts who use vague terms like "shared bodily fluids" and speak of "probabilities" and "percentages" instead of giving yes or no answers.

"This isn't mass hysteria, it's frightened, unified parents."

Concern is growing over the possible spread of AIDS in prisons. In Denver, nervous officials quarantined a 16-year-old, convicted of carrying a concealed weapon, because he had tested positive for the AIDS virus. He ate off disposable plates, which, along with his bed linen, were incinerated after being handled with gloves and double-bagged. Later tests showed he did not have the disease. In prisons where sodomy and drug use are commonplace, some inmates are fatalistic. Says Nadim Khoury, chief of health services for the California department of corrections: "They say, 'What more can happen to us? I'm sentenced for life.'"

Many AIDS victims have nowhere to go: they have been turned out of their homes by fearful roommates or families, and their money has been exhausted by heavy medical bills. The problem is especially poignant in the case of orphans and abandoned children; in Florida's Dade County, one of these youngsters with AIDS is being raised in a county hospital. In New York City, the Roman Catholic archdiocese tried to set up an AIDS shelter in an unused convent on the Upper West Side, but backed off when parishioners refused to send their children to the neighboring parochial school. The privately run AIDS Resource Center in Manhattan managed to find housing for 21 victims in four buildings, and persuaded the city to pick up part of the cost. At $700 a month, it is cheaper to house them in these apartments than to leave them in city hospitals (cost: at least $4,000 a week).

The search for housing can become blackly absurd. When an AIDS crisis center in Atlanta tried to rent a home for victims, real estate agents refused to help them. One even ordered the center's representative, who did not have AIDS, out of his car. "There's just too much I don't know about this disease," the panicked agent protested. "I have kids. I didn't know what you wanted this property for." The center finally found a house for AIDS victims by keeping their ailment secret.

Bounced around by unnerved officials, some AIDS sufferers have become pitiful nomads. Fabian Bridges, diagnosed in Houston as having AIDS, wandered to Indianapolis, where he was arrested for stealing a bicycle. When a local judge, John Downer, heard that Bridges had AIDS, he reached into his pocket, gave the defendant $20 and told deputies to put him on a bus for Cleveland. Bridges, 30, was supposed to visit his mother there. Instead, he took to the streets, where he began peddling sex. The city offered Bridges medical aid and lodging, but he drifted from one shelter to another before getting arrested on a street corner for disorderly conduct. Released, he was last reported heading for Houston to "pick up his van." Cleveland officials, who cannot find any legal authority to incarcerate him indefinitely, were noticeably relieved to hear that he had left town.

When their condition is found out, AIDS victims often encounter severe discrimination on the job. Hairdressers, barbers and food handlers are routinely fired. In New York, AIDS victims fired from their jobs have brought more than 150 cases of discrimination. All have been settled with back pay or reinstatement.

Some AIDS victims endure their ostracism with remarkable grace. A 34-year-old Memphis man, who has requested anonymity, whiles away his hours playing contract bridge at the M.A. Lightman Bridge Club. When other club members learned that he had AIDS, they began to avoid him. The management forced him to wear rubber surgical gloves. "I don't like this reaction because I happen to be the brunt of it," he says, "but I do understand it. A lot of people in the club are older, and they simply don't know how to take it. Their doctors have not helped by telling them not to get close to me." His presence "has been a nuisance," sighs the club director, Nate Silverstein, "even though he's been very, very nice about it. Personally, if people treated me the way they do him, I wouldn't show my face around this club anymore."

Many nurses and doctors have shown courage and compassion in caring for AIDS patients. But in big-city hospitals, patients are sometimes left unwashed, lying in their excrement, their food trays stacked outside the door. In Plainfield, N.J., Doris Williams, the foster mother of a four-year-old girl, recalls that nurses at first held and cooed over the child. "But as soon as we got the AIDS diagnosis, they were dressed up like 'Ghostbusters' in gloves and masks."

Some AIDS sufferers have become pitiful nomads.

Dentists are especially reluctant to treat AIDS victims. So great is the fear that some dentists have taken to wearing surgical gloves and masks with all patients. In some California communities, fire fighters and lifeguards use special equipment for mouth-to-mouth resuscitation.

Those who help AIDS sufferers sometimes become the targets of intimidation and violence. In September 1985, the Edmund D. Edelman Health Center of the Gay and Lesbian Community Services Center in Los Angeles received three bomb warnings, and its director, Hugh Rice, was threatened with death. In mid-September, a carload of people threw a vial of acid at a woman employee, burning her face, shoulder and arm. The victim said one of her attackers screamed, "Die, you AIDS faggots!"

Many gay activists fear that the stigma of AIDS will wipe out the almost two decades of progress in homosexual rights that began in the late 1960s. Tales of AIDS-related homophobia abound: in New York City, some diners avoid restaurants that have gay waiters. In Washington, D.C., a doctor requires gays to be tested for AIDS before he will give them hair transplants. In Louisville, city detectives donned rubber gloves before entering a gay bar to check for underage drinkers. Says Ken Vance, director of a gay counseling center in Houston: "It's going to get worse before it gets better. As more people become aware of AIDS, there will be a bigger backlash against gays."

The fear and uncertainty have at least in some cases spurred more public funding for research, care of AIDS patients and education programs. In Massachusetts, Governor Michael Dukakis budgeted $1.18 million for AIDS education in 1985. The federal appropriation for AIDS research jumped from $5.5 million in 1982 to $106.5 million in 1985. And in mid-September 1985 the Administration acknowledged the gravity of the disease when Vice President George Bush Sr. told the *San Francisco Chronicle* that AIDS was a "critical epidemic."

But government efforts have not been without controversy. After a gay group began distributing *Mother's Handy Sex Guide*, an explicit manual on "safe sex," at Los Angeles bath houses, gay bars and clinics, Los Angeles County Supervisor Peter Schabarum denounced the eight-page brochure as "plain, hard-core pornography." In August 1985, under his prodding, the Los Angeles County board of supervisors began to "review" its $1.1 million in funding for local gay community agencies.

More heartening is the example of San Francisco, one of the cities hit earliest and hardest by AIDS. (In September 1985 alone, 67 new cases were diagnosed, bringing the city's total since 1981 to 1,463.) There the scare stories have begun to disappear from the newspapers, and public panic had abated. "We're past the concern with casual contagion," says Holly Smith, spokeswoman for the San Francisco AIDS Foundation.

In mid-September 1985, San Francisco TV station KPIX aired an hour show called "Our Worst Fears: The AIDS Epidemic," which carefully explained what is known about the disease. The program was watched by nearly a million people, the largest audience ever for a public-service broadcast in the Bay Area. The Westinghouse Broadcasting system aired the program in Philadelphia, Baltimore, Pittsburgh and Boston as well. Says Boston's WBZ-TV Station

Manager Tom Goodgame: "The problem with AIDS is really two epidemics—the real health epidemic and the epidemic of the mind. We're trying to make some sense of the false rumors."

Nonetheless, the fear of the unknown that caused thousands of parents to keep their children home from school last week is bound to spread. After broadcasting a news story about the New York boycott, Memphis TV station WHBQ conducted a phone-in poll asking viewers, "Would you send your child to school with a child who has AIDS?" Results: 493 yes, 701 no.

The Queens neighborhoods where the boycott erupted are solid middle-class communities, very much like scores of neighborhoods all over the U.S. "I'm sure there are people in Tennessee who think this is just a big-city problem," said Mary Lorraine Napoli, who helped organize the boycott of P.S. 63. "But it's a worldwide problem. Why else have Swiss TV and the Canadian and Japanese press been here? It's not just our children we're worried about. It's everybody's."

3
The Federal Government's Response to AIDS Was Inadequate

Craig A. Rimmerman

In this selection, Craig A. Rimmerman presents his view that Ronald Reagan and George H.W. Bush, the Republican presidents of the 1980s, avoided the subject of AIDS as long as possible because, as a reputed disease of homosexuals, it was repugnant to them and to their New Right supporters. Reagan, Rimmerman says, apparently kept hoping that AIDS would "go away" and refused even to say the word publicly until 1987. Rimmerman claims that the Reagan administration opposed most funding for research on the disease and measures to halt discrimination against people who suffered from it. According to Rimmerman, Bush, elected in 1988, basically continued Reagan's policies in regard to the disease, although by 1990 he took a somewhat more sympathetic stance. Rimmerman, an expert in gay rights, youth activism, and the presidency, is a professor of political science at Hobart and William Smith Colleges in Geneva, New York. He has written many books, including *From Identity to Politics: The Lesbian and Gay Movements in the United States.*

Presidents [of the United States] frequently maintain a low profile with newly identified public health hazards. They often perceive that such concerns offer little political gain and many risks. Gerald Ford's 1976 announcement of the swine flu program was an exception. The response of

Excerpted from "Presidency, U.S.," by Craig A. Rimmerman, *The Encyclopedia of AIDS: A Social, Political, Cultural, and Scientific Record of the HIV Epidemic*, edited by Raymond A. Smith (Chicago: Fitzroy Dearborn Publishers, 1998).

Presidents Ronald Reagan and George Bush to AIDS fits the more general pattern of presidential caution in addressing public health concerns.

Avoiding a Risky Topic

For Reagan, AIDS presented a number of potentially serious political risks. As a presidential candidate, Reagan promised to eliminate the role of the federal government in the limited American welfare state, as well as to raise questions of morality and family in social policy. When AIDS was first reported in 1981, Reagan had recently assumed office and had begun to address the conservative agenda by slashing social programs and cutting taxes and by embracing conservative moral principles. As a result, Reagan never mentioned AIDS publicly until 1987. Most observers contend that AIDS research and public education were not funded adequately in the early years of the epidemic, at a time when research and public education could have saved lives.

In the early 1980s, senior officials from the Department of Health and Human Services pleaded for additional funding behind the scenes while they maintained publicly, for political reasons, that they had enough resources. The Reagan administration treated AIDS as a series of state and local problems rather than as a national problem. This helped to fragment the limited governmental response early in the AIDS epidemic.

Reagan thought of AIDS as though "it was measles and it would go away."

AIDS could not have struck at a worse time politically. With the election of Reagan in 1980, the "New Right" in American politics ascended. Many of those who assumed power embraced political and personal beliefs hostile to gay men and lesbians. Health officials, failing to educate about transmission and risk behavior, undermined any chance of an accurate public understanding of AIDS. The new conservatism also engendered hostility toward those with AIDS. People with AIDS (PWAs) were scapegoated and stigmatized. It was widely reported, as well, that New Right groups, such as the Moral Majority, successfully prevented funding for AIDS education programs and counseling services for PWAs. At various points in the epidemic, conservatives called for the quarantining and tattooing of PWAs. Jerry Falwell, the leader of the Moral Majority, was quoted as stating: "AIDS is the wrath of God upon homosexuals."

This larger conservative climate enabled the Reagan administration's indifference toward AIDS. The administration undercut federal efforts to confront AIDS in a meaningful way by refusing to spend the money Congress allocated for AIDS research. In the critical years of 1984 and 1985, according to his White House physician Reagan thought of AIDS as though "it was measles and it would go away." Reagan's biographer Lou Cannon claims that thc president's response to AIDS was "halting and ineffective." It took [actor] Rock Hudson's death from AIDS in 1985 to prompt Reagan to change his personal views, although members of his administration were still openly hostile to more aggressive government funding of research and public education. Six years after the onset of the epidemic, Reagan finally mentioned the word "AIDS" publicly at the Third International AIDS Conference held in Washington, D.C. Reagan's only concrete proposal at this time was widespread routine testing.

Muzzling the Surgeon General

Reagan and his close political advisers also successfully prevented his surgeon general, C. Everett Koop, from discussing AIDS publicly until Reagan's second term. Congress mandates that the surgeon general's chief responsibility is to promote the health of the American people and to inform the public about the prevention of disease. In the Reagan administration, however, the surgeon general's central role was to promote the administration's conservative social agenda, especially pro-life and family issues.

At a time when the surgeon general could have played an invaluable role in public health education, Koop was prevented from even addressing AIDS publicly. Then, in February 1986, Reagan asked Koop to write a report on the AIDS epidemic. Koop had come to the attention of conservatives in the Reagan administration because of his leading role in the anti-abortion movement. Reagan administration officials fully expected Koop to embrace conservative principles in his report on AIDS.

When the *Surgeon General's Report on Acquired Immune*

Deficiency Syndrome was released to the public on October 22, 1986, it was a call for federal action in response to AIDS, and it underscored the importance of a comprehensive AIDS education strategy, beginning in grade school. Koop advocated the widespread distribution of condoms and concluded that mandatory identification of people with HIV or any form of quarantine would be useless in addressing AIDS. As part of Koop's broad federal education strategy, the Public Health Service sent AIDS mailers to 107 million American households. Koop's actions brought him into direct conflict with William Bennett, Reagan's secretary of education. Bennett opposed Koop's recommendations and called for compulsory HIV testing of foreigners applying for immigration visas, for marriage license applicants, for all hospital patients, and for prison inmates.

The Reagan administration did little to prohibit HIV/AIDS discrimination.

The Reagan administration did little to prohibit HIV/AIDS discrimination. The administration placed responsibility for addressing AIDS discrimination issues with the states rather than with the federal government. In the face of federal inaction, some states and localities passed laws that prohibited HIV/AIDS discrimination. It took the Supreme Court, in its 1987 *School Board of Nassau County, Fla. v. Arline* decision, to issue a broad ruling that was widely interpreted as protecting those with HIV or AIDS from discrimination in federal executive agencies, in federally assisted programs or activities, or by businesses with federal contracts.

Reagan did appoint the Presidential Commission on the Human Immunodeficiency Virus Epidemic in the summer of 1987; it was later renamed the Watkins Commission, after its chair. With the appointment of this commission, Reagan was able to appease those who demanded a more sustained federal response to AIDS. He also answered the concerns of the New Right by appointing an AIDS commission that included few scientists who had participated in AIDS research and few physicians who had actually treated PWAs. In addition, the commission included outspoken opponents of AIDS education.

In retrospect, it is clear that the commission was created to deflect attention from the administration's own inept policy response to AIDS. The Watkins Commission's final report did recommend a more sustained federal commitment to address AIDS, but this recommendation was largely ignored by both the Reagan and Bush administrations. None of the commissions studying AIDS over the years has recommended a massive federal effort to confront AIDS at all levels of society.

A Stronger Response

As Reagan's vice president in 1987, George Bush Sr. nominally headed the AIDS Executive Committee of the National Institutes of Health. Bush also had to balance his roles as Reagan's adviser with his role as a presidential candidate in the 1988 election. In doing so, Bush appealed to the New Right by endorsing policies that would publicly identify people who were HIV-positive and that required mandatory HIV tests when people applied for marriage licenses. On the 1988 presidential campaign trail, Bush argued that HIV testing is more cost-effective than spending money on treatment. After Bush was elected president in 1988, it came as no surprise that he continued most of the policies of the Reagan era. Bush did appear, however, to be more sensitive to the magnitude of the AIDS crisis.

In terms of public policy, the Bush administration continued Reagan's fiscal austerity with respect to AIDS. In addition, Bush embraced mandatory testing to prevent the spread of AIDS. Finally, his administration argued that local officials should design and implement AIDS educational strategies, although federal resources could be used to gather more AIDS information. His surgeon general, Antonia Novello, maintained a low profile on AIDS issues.

It was not until March 30, 1990, almost nine years after AIDS was first identified and over a year into his presidency, that George Bush gave his first speech on AIDS. He praised his administration's efforts in dealing with the AIDS crisis and asked the country to end discrimination against those infected with HIV. At the same time, Bush refused to eliminate a federal policy that placed restrictions on HIV-positive foreigners who wished to enter the United States. The speech was heralded as the strongest public commitment ever articulated by a president, even though most AIDS activists argued that it was the kind of speech that should have been given in the early 1980s. Bush was criticized for not endorsing a comprehensive federal policy for addressing AIDS and for perpetuating discrimination against HIV-positive individuals who wished to enter the United States. However, Bush did sign the Ryan White Comprehensive AIDS Resource Emergency (CARE) Act into law in 1990, although he consistently opposed funding this legislation to the degree its congressional supporters requested. The legislation was originally designed to provide federal assistance for urban areas that were hardest hit by AIDS.

The Federal Government's Response to AIDS Was Adequate

Kenneth W. Sell, interviewed by Victoria A. Harden

Kenneth W. Sell was scientific director of the National Institute of Allergy and Infectious Diseases (NIAID), part of the National Institutes of Health (NIH), in the early 1980s, and was in charge of allocating resources to fight new infectious diseases such as AIDS. In this excerpt from an interview conducted on November 3, 1988, by Victoria A. Harden, director of the NIH Historical Office, Sell maintains that both the NIH and Congress responded quickly and adequately to the need for research on the mysterious new epidemic. He denies that anyone held back on research because the disease was associated with homosexuality. The interview was part of an oral history project in which NIH researchers involved with AIDS during the early years of the epidemic described their experiences. Dr. Sell died in October 1996.

Victoria Harden: There have been many criticisms in the press and in books that the response to AIDS was too slow. Many people seemed to express the attitude that scientists should have had instant communications and instant answers. I think it's important that you believe that progress against AIDS was not slow.

Kenneth W. Sell: My own view is that from the early days we progressed as fast as anyone had a good idea to sup-

Excerpted from "Interview with Dr. Kenneth W. Sell," by Victoria A. Harden, http://aidshistory.nih.gov, National Institute of Health, November 3, 1988.

port. Ideas that came from the outside in response to our RFPs and RFAs [Request for Proposals; Request for Applications] were funded at a payline level much lower than anything else we were planning at NIH—that is, the scientific merit of these proposals, as judged by the study sections reviewing them, could be much lower than usual grants and still be funded. That decision was an obvious attempt to try to get resources committed to the problem.

The afflicted are . . . driving for things that cannot be done.

I totally disagree with people who say things didn't progress rapidly. Our understanding of the disease, the agent, and the epidemiology developed more rapidly than any other new infection in the history of biomedical sciences. It's a serious epidemic and, therefore, wanting to know all the answers immediately is understandable, but blaming the scientific community for not progressing fast enough is totally irresponsible.

Furthermore, I never saw anyone refraining from the pursuit of this scientific investigation because they thought that the people at risk weren't worth studying. This is another claim that's made sometimes. I certainly never saw that attitude the entire time I worked closely with the problem, and I worked quite a few years at National Institute of Allergy and Infectious Diseases (NIAID). It just never came up and was never even hinted at. That isn't to say there isn't a single scientist anywhere who is anti-gay, but I never saw that at National Institutes of Health (NIH).

Responsible Reactions

Your funding came from Congress, which influenced what you could do with your resources. Do you think that Congress, the administration, and the public understand well enough how biomedical science works, and if not, how can scientists get the message across?

I think Congress really does understand that basic science is important. The people in Congress that I spoke to understood that it was basic science that allowed us to understand this disease as early as we did. We understood the disease because we knew the immune system. Congress is relatively sophisticated, and even though members like to target money towards pet projects, they understand that basic science—R01 grants, fundamental research—is very important. I think we need to harp on that constantly, but they have an amazing amount of understanding.

There was an amazing amount of understanding in the public from the very earliest time. I felt there was a lot of responsible reporting about AIDS very early on. Almost weekly we had somebody in the office talking about AIDS, ranging from people at the U.S. television networks to those from newspapers. The vast majority of the reporting was very responsibly done. It's amazing how much good information comes out over the TV and in the press when the media deal with this subject. This responsible reporting has led the majority of the population to understand this particular disease, what's going on and the need for all kinds of research, not just treatment trials.

Dangerous Demands

The people who are afflicted have bombarded the press with the need for instant cures, instant answers, instant vaccines, and immediate access to drugs that haven't been proven yet. The afflicted are the ones who are really driving for things that cannot be done. They are driving for answers that we don't have. They are driving for drugs to be used that aren't available or have not even been adequately tested for safety. It's understandable to do that if you have a disease that's 100 percent fatal. When people with cancer get to a stage that's 100 percent fatal, they do the same thing, just perhaps not so vocally. It's understandable. But I think that the general public understands the disease reasonably well, although it always bothers me when I see kids being ostracized in school because of ignorance in some families. At the same time I see many school districts turning around and welcoming those kids into their schools. Many parents and various school officials do understand. There are always a few misguided, but the understanding of the disease is pretty remarkable.

Following up on your comments about drugs, I recall a reporter's asking me whether scientists were trying to hold up the release of potential therapeutic drugs from people with AIDS. I replied that I thought it was a regulatory question, that the Congress had decided that the U.S. would not permit people to mar-

ket drugs without testing for safety and efficacy. Clinical trials, of course, take a long time. Is there any other way rather than having a proper clinical trial to tell if a drug is working?

Even when you have a proper clinical trial it's often difficult to know what value any particular drug is. I don't think any scientist is holding up anything. The regulatory agency [Food and Drug Administration] wants to be shown that one drug is better than another. It's the safety of the public that's important. There's also a huge financial burden. Take a look at what the federal government has paid for AZT [3'-Azido-2',3'-dideoxythiamidine]. If we didn't have some data indicating it really did some good, it would be an incredible rip-off of society, of people dying with AIDS.

The primary concern about drugs is the safety of the individual. Even if people with AIDS are dying, that does not mean we should hasten their death or make their existence more unbearable. Even AZT has a huge problem with bone marrow depression and the need for blood transfusions. It's not an innocuous drug, and yet we're talking about using drugs that are more toxic but that we don't know much about. There's tremendous pressure from those who are dying to try anything, and there is pressure from the regulatory agency saying we can't approve everything. We have to have at least some modicum of knowledge about the drug before we let the public use it. I don't think any scientist has held anything back in terms of treatment of patients. In fact, the doctors and the scientists are pushing on the patients' side. They're willing to try almost anything they can get their hands on to help the patients, because they feel just as helpless as the patients do.

5

AIDS Activism Helped the Gay Community

Benjamin Heim Shepard

Benjamin Heim Shepard, a social worker who became a social historian, worked for two years as a counselor at one of San Francisco's largest AIDS housing programs. He interviewed 30 persons with AIDS (PWAs) around 1995 to create an oral history of the AIDS epidemic in San Francisco. In this excerpt from that oral history, White Nights and Ascending Shadows, *Shepard interviews five HIV-positive AIDS activists, including G'dali Braverman, who formerly played a major role in the AIDS Coalition to Unleash Power (ACT UP), one of the best known radical AIDS activist organizations, in New York. The activists describe what drew them to the activist cause, what it felt like to take part in demonstrations, and the good that they believe AIDS activism did for the gay community and others. Shepard has also written* A War of Nerves: Soldiers and Psychiatrists in the Twentieth Century.

"The two most famous quotes in activist folklore are Joe Hill's 'Don't mourn, organize' and Mother Jones's 'Pray for the dead, but fight like hell for the living.' Although the latter makes a nod at acknowledging the dead, both place the emphasis on political action," Michael Bronski wrote about living in a United States with its selective compassion toward the dying. As the inaction of the Reagan era wore on, G'dali Braverman crossed a fundamental Rubicon [made a life-changing decision] leading to [joining] the AIDS Coalition to Unleash Power (ACT UP) New York in 1988. The

Excerpted from *White Nights and Ascending Shadows: An Oral History of the San Francisco AIDS Epidemic*, by Benjamin Heim Shepard (Herndon, VA: Cassell, 1997).

battle against the health care establishment he would engage in with ACT UP would help all Americans. If AIDS activists had not hung in there screaming, "We're here! We're Queer! And we're sick!" it's hard to imagine the health care debates of the 1990s occurring. Cleve Jones put the era in context.

"We're here! We're Queer! And we're sick!"

Cleve Jones So there was this first big wave [of AIDS activism in the early 1980s] and that was followed by a second angrier wave in the late '80s that gave birth to ACT UP, the Names Project, World AIDS Day, sort of grass-roots political or semi-political actions. I think one of the things that's been confusing for many people is that the Gay/Lesbian Movement and the AIDS movement, I don't really think of the AIDS movement as movement. I think of the Gay and Lesbian Movement as a Civil Rights, as a sexual liberation movement and then you have a response to the epidemic and they become intertwined. People have trouble, I think, keeping them separate. Very different people are driving those two. You still have a lot of people like myself who think of ourselves as Gay Liberationists. Now, you also have a majority of people who are in the movement who don't come from that perspective at all and who have come out in the late 1980s and early 1990s. And it's odd for me to watch it sometimes. . . .

A Focus of Energy

G'dali Braverman I think the root of AIDS activism necessited our looking at issues around basic gay homophobia to begin to identify why the world wasn't facing up to AIDS. We were not an organized community. We were invisible. We were narcissistic. We pursued our basic primal needs without really thinking, "What is the future direction of our community politically, locally, state-wide, nationally?" You have, basically, masses of people who are closeted or hiding who aren't going to identify themselves under almost any circumstance and accept that risk, even when they are dying. They didn't want to have to deal with the phobias around their sexuality or lifestyle. There was a negative support structure for creating a working environment around the disease.

I met a guy in '87. We were in a relationship for the better part of '87, '88. I had received a couple of flyers in the mail about ACT UP. I breezed through them and, basically, tossed them. I was feeling that I was in this relationship with a generally vacuous person who really didn't seem to have any great concern for the world around him besides how good he looked and which club he was going to. When ACT UP passed we stood on the sidewalk, at the Gay Pride Parade in 1988, a year after its formation, I took one look and said, "I am going to go to the next meeting of that organization." There was a sense of power, a sense of action. It didn't appear to be about pity or shame or sadness or guilt. It seemed to be about anger and action. I think that as the individual that I am and as a Jew those were things that I could identify with. So I dumped him, picked up ACT UP.

There was a sense of power, a sense of action.

My first meeting was right after Gay Pride. It was on the first floor and it was packed. People flooded out the doors. People were in the hallways. There was no ventilation. But there was the sense that this was the place to be, all the energy, all the focus around HIV was happening in that room. And I just listened. It was probably young gay men mostly, twenty-three to thirty-five, physically fit, an exceptionally large number of attractive people, energetic, articulate people. Probably 30 to 40 percent of the organization was composed of Jews. Jews have always been at the center of leftist movements which have always ended up fucking them over in the end. An agenda was put together. The meeting went on for three and half hours and people stayed. All ages, sixteen to sixty, the whole gamut. Men, women, boys, girls, parents, but mostly gay men and you didn't know who was HIV-positive or not.

Even from that early time there were only a few of us who identified as positive. I was one of those people. I found out in early '87. I don't remember it definitely. By that time I had accepted the fact that chances were that everybody I knew was going to die and that I was going to die and it was just a question of time. It just seemed the logical conclusion. In retrospect it *was*.

Actions were proposed every week at that point. I can

remember feeling a buzz in those earlier demonstrations. I'd be leaving my office or my apartment and walking or being on a subway and having this sense of the unknown in my gut, this feeling that I was putting myself at risk and this response circulating through my blood of "You have to! You must. This is just something that you are going to do" and hearing myself think, "What's going to happen? Is there going to be brutality? Are people going to be fighting? Is there going to be a confrontation? What is my response going to be? Am I going to be able to stick to our non-violent guidelines? Am I not going to feel a need to reciprocate aggression on a physical level?" As a new person you go through this constant inner checks and balances because you are so filled with a fury. We helped perpetuate that anger in the discussions that we had around the actions so that you are a bottle of emotions with a great sense of purpose. When you were at the demonstration you sustained yourself on an adrenaline rush because you were chanting the whole time whether it was a half an hour or an hour and a half. Physically maintaining that energy level does incredible things to you. You walk away from the demonstration feeling elated, really elated and purposeful. I don't think that I ever experienced an overwhelming fear. I always had a sense that I have a good head on my shoulders and that I would know how to respond and react in critical situations.

I, early on, chose to be visible in my work and to take a sort of leadership role in my work as an AIDS activist. I still didn't socialize with AIDS activists, didn't sleep with AIDS activists, didn't seek to establish friendships, and didn't seek out media interviews, but I sought to be central on issues that I chose to work on.

Housing, Treatment, and City Issues

ACT UP was working on a multitude of issues. There were probably a good twenty committees existing, treatment issues, housing, local issues, city issues, a media committee, etc. There were people working on those issues that were meeting several times a week outside of the regular Monday meeting.

I chose to work on housing for general reasons that it would be difficult to muster people to work on an issue that wasn't a glamorous issue. The committee had just been formed the previous week. The issues the floor was responsive to at that point were local issues and treatment issues around the Food and Drug Administration (FDA) and the National Institutes of Health (NIH). Housing would be difficult because here we were predominantly middle-class to affluent gay men whose self-perception would be that one would probably never have to deal with becoming destitute and therefore this seemed like a peripheral issue. We would be advocating for mostly a minority population. I thought it would be a challenge to get these organizations to deal with their issues. We turned out to be a very successful committee and mustered large attendance at our demonstrations.

When you were at [a] demonstration you sustained yourself on an adrenaline rush.

The first demonstration that I was involved with was at the Trump Tower on Fifth Avenue targeting Donald Trump and New York City for the millions of dollars in tax rebates that developers like him were receiving. We felt these funds should be going towards low-income housing and the abolition of shelters as primary housing for homeless people and inappropriate housing for homeless people with life-threatening illnesses. We moved on to having several successful demonstrations against the city's Housing Preservation and Development and Housing Works departments. They were very successful demonstrations, in terms of the media pull and getting the public officials to the table to negotiate, and in terms of getting any community response around issues. I think we really were instrumental in the early work that transcended the issues around being a gay man with HIV. After I left New York to come to San Francisco the committee actually went on to develop an organization called Housing Works which provides housing . . . .

Don't Go Quietly

Brad Sherbert My circle of friends keeps changing 'cause people die. I don't know what keeps me here so long; I see people doing everything they can to take as much care of their body as possible and they still die very fast. I can remember and I go to the funeral and I just go on. It wasn't too long ago when I used to get real nervous in front of a crowd of people to give a eulogy. Hell, I've had so much practice at it now, I oughta have one gigantic eulogy speech for everybody and just fill in the name (*laughs*). It doesn't make me nervous or anything anymore. It's really hard too. You don't really get used to it but you become accustomed to it. It's the worst thing, I think this epidemic, that anybody could imagine.

Of course I went with ACT UP to City Hall [in San Francisco in the late 1980s]. And we spent the whole day in City Hall raising hell. I got there at ten in the morning and finally at four in the afternoon I got arrested. We didn't know at what time the city supervisors were going to meet. We were going to stay there until we got arrested or they met. Finally they met and, it's like, I sat up and started screaming about the budget cuts and people dying. I told them, "This disease is killing me." And I said, "If you don't allocate money here, here and here, I'm gonna die sooner than I have to." And the one supervisor, I forget her name, Angela Allioto, she's supposed to be our friend. She's like, "Sir, if you'll just take a seat and be quiet, you'll get your turn to speak." And I'm like, "Look, I've been here all day and you're here. That'll affect, how long I will live depends on how much money you allocate and you're telling me to sit down and shut up." I said, "Hell no, I'm not going to sit down and shut up." I kept right on talking and she motioned to the cops, OK come get him.

I became an AIDS activist because I felt that the whole system was corrupt.

They put the little plastic handcuffs on me. And, of course, it didn't hurt, they put them fairly loose and stuff and I like kicked and yelled that they were hurting me and screamed (*laughs*). I did not go easily. That's because, if you go peaceably, you don't draw any attention. Well they carted this guy off to jail—but if you make a scene? That night I was on every channel. I was on the front page of the *Chronicle* paper, the front page of the *Bay Area Reporter*. That's what happens when you throw a fit when you get arrested. You go peacefully, they don't even mention it on the news. (*Sardonically.*) The news media reported it as a slightly noisy demonstration (*laughs*). I bet nobody got any work done at City Hall that day, OK.

I'm surprised they didn't arrest me sooner. We had the city supervisors' office blocked off at one point. And it was like, one guy came and said, "I just want to come and get a few of these papers." And I said, "You know what I think of these papers." There was like a stack about two feet tall of all these different forms. I grabbed the whole stack. Took it out of the supervisors main office, went out to the balcony inside City Hall and just tossed the shit as hard as I could. And I said, "That's what I think about all this red tape bullshit!" I thought for sure I was going to jail when I did that. I thought, God this is too wild to pull this shit and get away with it, you know.

Philosophy of an Activist

G'dali Braverman There's a point when there's a demonstration where my mother will call me from New York and if I pick up the phone she will say, "I can't believe you are out of jail already. I thought I'd, you know, would leave a message on your voice-mail just saying, 'call me when you get home later.'" I'm not blasé about the importance of civil disobedience and the importance of risking arrest to get your message across. It's just part of my responsibility as an activist.

I can honestly say that I didn't become an AIDS activist to save my life. I didn't have that as an ulterior motive. I became an AIDS activist because I felt that the whole system was corrupt and that our government was at fault for the spread of this disease and that we needed to wake up. It was about the world. It really was about the world and about our world as a gay people, which I still recognize and believe will be annihilated because of this epidemic. As our community becomes more passive, more reticent, I can see those AIDS activists who are left saying that old adage, "Help yourself first so you can help others." Many of us are at a mid- to late stage of disease where if we don't survive and there aren't any new people coming into it, then we can't do anything to help future generations. Ultimately that hasn't been my objective. My philosophy is that this epidemic will be with us for at least another generation and therefore we should do everything in our power to keep the urgency of AIDS focused in the public eye . . . .

When we left a demonstration in the early days we had this sort of unspoken understanding that we would gather, those of us that had been arrested. Or some of us would gather in groups, go get something to eat, or hang out at someone's house, or spend the rest of the day together because of the crash. The emotional crash that comes afterwards is intense because for those instants of the demonstration you forget that you're not living at the tail end of an epidemic. You forget that everything that you are demanding is not going to be achieved when the demonstration is over. You are so focused on the moment that you, somewhere in your mind, believe that the solution is here, in the action and clearly it isn't. This is just part of the process. So when you end up home alone afterwards, you wake up to the fact that death is still here, your friends are still dying, you're still sick, the system still exists as it was and that some changes may come about but it's just the beginning. One of the difficult things of being an activist is maintaining that high level of energy and motivation and not letting the crashes destroy you. My crashes were always short-lived 'cause I was always so busy organizing another project. I think in the late 1980s, particularly in New York, there were so many people and there was such camaraderie that it was easy to stay focused and to feel a sense of support. With the attrition in the mid-1990s, that doesn't exist.

Beyond AIDS

Dan Vojir The ends are very noble. I used to get upset at ACT UP. I think they've calmed down bit. I think they've done a lot for people. In fact, there was one woman I was talking to. Her child has Down's Syndrome [a birth defect causing developmental disability]. She's practically reversed the Down's Syndrome in the child by using certain smart drugs. She said, "You know something, if it weren't for ACT UP, my kid wouldn't be alive today." I says, "Why?" because her child didn't have HIV. She says because it was ACT UP that got the FDA to accept the mail order drugs that we finally get in the country. She says, "I totally support everything ACT UP ever does because of what they did for my child actually, inadvertently." She says, "A lot of people don't know that ACT UP did a hell of a lot of stuff for a lot of other people who don't have AIDS."

Jay Segal You only do drugs [take anti-AIDS drugs] for one reason and that is to stall the progression of the disease until a cure comes along. Realistically, you're not going to see the cure, not for about another forty years, maybe. I've learned a lot about AIDS, joined both groups of ACT UP, got things changed. They're the only people on this planet that have made any changes. Congress wouldn't have changed on its own. The President wouldn't have done anything on his own. I don't always agree with them but they work. This country was built on activism. Look at the Boston Tea Party, talk about a major demo. They took a whole bay. We just trashed ships. And ACT UP is good activism. The cause is good.

I was heavy into ACT UP in Chicago. Dealt with a couple of major demos on health care and alternatives. The Chicago Demo, I was significant in that one in its inception and creation. ACT UP is a bunch of sick sissies who can't agree on anything that somehow get a lot of work done. Strangely enough, in almost every major AIDS conference that's ever going to happen in 1995, ACT UP is on the committees, ACT UP is on the speakers lists. ACT UP is a reputable source now because they've dealt with it more. They are personally impacted.

A Fabulous Moment

Cleve Jones I produced all the candlelight marches for the first eleven years. The tenth anniversary of the murders of Harvey Milk and George Moscone. In 1988, [in San Francisco], I woke in the middle of the night, Oh, I know exactly how to do this this year. And I came up with this scenario that I would have a bare stage with a single spot. As we started with candles and I had the stage be totally dark and then without any announcement, a single spotlight, I wanted Joan Baez to walk out on stage and without any other words to sing, "I dreamed I saw Joe Hill last night, alive as you and me, I said Joe you're ten years dead, I never died said he, I never died said he." And I called her up and she said, "Oh, yes, that would be fabulous." And she did it. There's been about a half dozen times in my life where I saw something so clearly and then got to see it just as I'd imagined. She came out. The crowd recognized her before she got to the microphone, but her voice was so distinctive they knew it and there was an electricity through the crowd. It was Joan Baez and she was singing this great labor song that applied to our situation and had this thread of continuity. It was faaaabulous!!!

AIDS Activism Hurt the Gay Community

Darrell Yates Rist

Darrell Yates Rist, himself a gay activist with AIDS, nonetheless argues in this 1989 article that an "obsession" with AIDS is hurting the gay community by distracting it from other equally important issues, such as the needs of gay youth, violence against gays, laws against gay marriage, and the lack of gay civil rights. Although Rist agrees that AIDS activism and the gay civil rights movements often overlap, he maintains that their politics are sometimes incompatible. Rist, who died of AIDS in 1993, was an actor, director, and associate producer as well as an author of screenplays, articles for *Nation* and other magazines, and a book, *Heartlands: A Gay Man's Odyssey Across America.*

> In seasons of pestilence, some of us will have a secret attraction to the disease—a terrible passing inclination to die of it—And all of us have like wonders hidden in our breasts, only needing circumstances to evoke them. —Charles Dickens, *A Tale of Two Cities*

In the mid-1980s, while I was researching a book on the lives of gay men across America, a writer friend offered me an unsettling view of gay San Francisco. Rob Goldstein had no use for the polish and smugness of the Castro [an area of San Francisco where many gay men live], the Promised Land for homosexuals; he toured me instead through the disenfranchised Latino gay life of the Mission district and the destitution of the Tenderloin. In the Tenderloin, I met homeless gay men with AIDS and gay teen-

From "AIDS as Apocalypse: The Deadly Costs of an Obsession," by Darrell Yates Rist, *Nation*, February 13, 1989.

age runaways who risked their lives bartering sex for meals and drugs, hustling on every street corner.

I had just spent a night among those abandoned adolescents when, at a dinner in the Castro, I listened to the other guests talk about nothing but AIDS, the dead, the dying—which to their minds included every gay man in the city: fashionable hysteria. "This," one of them actually said, "is the only thing worth fighting for." Not long before, I'd heard Larry Kramer, playwright and AIDS activist, say something like that too, and had felt, in that suffocating moment, that finally we'd all gone suicidal, that we'd die of our own death wish.

Though I tried above all to empathize with my tablemates' wretchedness, the other images of San Francisco kept importuning. I described what I'd seen in their hometown and recalled the gay youth agency I knew best, New York City's Hetrick-Martin Institute, its dreary facilities, small staff and paltry budget. "Shouldn't we start worrying again about all those issues we've forgotten in the epidemic? Gay kids?" I ventured—as though we'd ever really cared. "Even if they don't get AIDS, what are we giving them to live for?"

The guests fell silent. Across from me sat an elder of the city's gay community, a man of money and influence. He stared at me in utter disbelief, his face suspended above the pork. "How can we?" he replied "We're dying!"

An Unjustified Obsession

There's an oily sentiment among gay men and Lesbians in the late 1980s that—amid the din of a culture that keeps us in our place—we've matured; that we've grown aggressive in defense of our lives since fate, with some harsh wisdom, sent us AIDS. We produce abundant evidence of sacrifice to prove the claim: For most of the 1980s we've frantically been building AIDS organizations, draining our pockets poor with AIDS donations, exhausting our strength as AIDS volunteers, doing battle with AIDS bigots, creating mayhem in the streets, nurturing, mourning, worrying about infection till we're sick, dying with a desperate hold on dignity. We've been full of AIDS—gay men, Lesbians, our parents, our newly sympathetic heterosexual friends. We've all had heart, in fact, for nothing else.

Even Lesbians, none of whom, according to the U.S.

Centers for Disease Control (C.D.C.), have contracted AIDS making love to a woman, have taken to keening that the whole gay community is dying—so compulsive is the human need to partake in the drama of catastrophe. And this panicky faith that all of us are doomed cries down the sobering truth that it is only a minority of homosexuals who've been stricken or ever will be, leaving the rest of us to confront not so much the grief of dying as the bitterness, in an oppressive world, of staying alive.

"Shouldn't we start worrying again about all those issues we've forgotten in the epidemic?"

No one has influenced (or parroted) the gay community's views on AIDS more than Larry Kramer and his organizational offspring, New York's AIDS Coalition to Unleash Power (ACT UP)—chic street protesters with clones, albeit autonomous ones, in nearly every major city. The numbers they use to pronounce universal death on the gay community's men are immoral because they are panic-mongering, insidious because they are specious. They fall within some extreme theoretical realm of possibility, and therefore prey on the frightened; they willfully propagate the worst that medical science can imagine, regardless of the improbability, regardless of maddening contradictions in epidemiologic definitions and data.

Neither Kramer nor anyone else has any hard national figures on the prevalence of infection with HIV, the virus assumed to cause AIDS. But most activists, and the media, seem to have swallowed the C.D.C.'s estimate of 1 million to 1.5 million men, women and children. These numbers, unchanged from 1986 to 1989 despite the luridly publicized "spread" of HIV, ludicrously derive not from national seroprevalence surveys [surveys to determine the number of people infected with HIV] but in great part from mythical assumptions about the population size and sexual practices of gay men. Nevertheless, both Kramer's crowd and the media continue to broadcast the notion that HIV infection is uniformly fatal, even though the C.D.C.'s own Kung Jong Lui and William Darrow, on whose research the morbid dogma is based, have disavowed such sweeping prognoses as egregious misapplications of their work. Their San Francisco study, published in the June 3, 1988, issue of *Science*, suggested only that, among a small and very high-risk group of HIV antibody-positive men, there was a 90 percent probability that between 39 percent and 100 percent would develop AIDS—a crap shoot in statistics, one never intended to be a prediction.

More hopeful yet, the New York Blood Center's head epidemiologist, Dr. Cladd Stevens, has found that 20 to 25 percent of the HIV antibody-positive men she studied for ten years show no measurable immune dysfunction. Yet an article in *The Washington Post* on HIV infection, "AIDS Virus Likely Fatal to All Infected," chose, like most media reports, to misinterpret hysterically Lui and Darrow's study. And it is such terrifyingly irresponsible misanalyses of the San Francisco numbers that Kramer and his disciples embrace. Members of ACT UP have even passed out copies of the *Post* article in the streets, like biblical tracts.

According to the 1948 Alfred Kinsey statistics—old, but the most reliable figures we have—American men whose homosexuality is "more than incidental" make up 13 to 38 percent of the male population. In 1989, that's between 11.2 million and 32.8 million men. For the sake of argument, let's accept the C.D.C.'s top figure of 1.5 million people who would test positive for HIV in the United States. Let's even assume that all of them are homosexuals—ignoring the hundreds of thousands who are heterosexual intravenous drug users, hemophiliacs, heterosexually infected women, infected babies. Even if all 1.5 million died off in a biologically improbable holocaust, a minimum of 9.7 million homosexually active men and 5.6 million Lesbians (from Kinsey's 1983 statistic of minimum incidence of 6 percent homosexuality among women) would remain uninfected and sentenced to life.

The epidemic of violence has been long, brutal and often fatal.

Data on the homosexual population and AIDS will change in time and yield more truth—or less. But no imprecision in the numbers has sobered the gay apocalyptics for a moment. And their fantasy of wholesale mortality gives us yet a new excuse to desert the business of living and ignore the most vulnerable among us. Certainly when it comes to kids, even the homosexual heart for AIDS beats false; it beats only for men of a certain age, a certain color—in fact, a certain social class.

Neglected Gay Causes

Since its founding in 1981, New York's pre-eminent AIDS service organization, the Gay Men's Health Crisis (G. M. H. C.), with an annual budget of almost $11 million and $1 million more in material donations for new office furnishings in 1988 has never funded outreach of any kind to gay and Lesbian youth. I've been told again and again the organization is fearful of being accused of proselytizing, that most vicious imputation afflicting homosexuals. So children die while we dance to the songs of bigots. The Hetrick-Martin Institute makes its services available to the 150,000 gay and Lesbian adolescents that it estimates live in New York City. This group does provide AIDS outreach, but also administers a high school for homosexual kids harassed out of public schools, educates parents and teachers, runs support groups, conducts counseling, furnishes food, clothing and access to shelter to the adolescent homeless—almost all of whom are black or Latino. The institute had a staff in the 1987–1988 fiscal year of only twenty-four (including street counselors) and a mere $755,000 budget, most of which came from the city and state. Only 18 percent of the money came from the generosity of homosexual men and women and their friends, whereas nearly three-quarters of G.M.H.C.'s budget in 1989 comes from private donations and interest on the investment of excess income.

But even concerns more immediate than gay children fail to engage our self-interest. The battle against anti-gay violence languishes while assaults have soared specifically as a backlash to the disease. According to the New York City Gay and Lesbian Anti-Violence Project (A.V.P.), in the city alone there were 609 reported queer-bashings in 1988, reflecting a more than 300 percent increase since 1984, when AIDS stories began to saturate the media. Moreover, the A.V.P. reports that 90 percent of anti-gay and -lesbian crimes nationwide are never reported: Victims are afraid of being forced from the closet and demeaned by the police or made to face, in many states, the legally sanctioned discrimination of sodomy laws. Despite New York's huge gay and Lesbian population at risk of assault, the A.V.P. could muster a budget last year of a mere $150,000, just $10,000 of which was donated by the community.

The epidemic of violence has been long, brutal and often fatal. David Wertheimer, director of A.V.P., describes the hatred vented in anti-gay attacks as "unimaginable." Speaking about a series of murders in New York's Chelsea neighborhood that began in 1985, he said, "The victim is commonly found stabbed twenty or thirty times, sometimes with his castrated penis stuffed in his mouth." Yet there has not been a sustained outcry from the gay community against this violence.

Why are we so callous about these attacks? Can no threat but AIDS ignite our indignation? Why do we care so little, in fact, even for the sanctity of our relationships? Why is there no ACT UP specifically to protest laws forbidding same-sex marriage, banned in every state? Why no marathon protests at marriage license bureaus, no sit-ins at state legislatures, no class action suits? Why doesn't such brutality against our love incite our anger? Are we such demoralized creatures that only the threat of extinction can stir our collective will? When a car wreck left Sharon Kowalski a quadraplegic, her homophobic father had her quarantined by a court from Karen Thompson, her lover. Is the murder of their relationship at the hands of American law less of a horror than losing one's lover to a virus?

Incompatible Politics

In the late 1980s, for the first time since the onslaught of the AIDS epidemic in the early 1980s, one crucial organization, the National Gay and Lesbian Task Force, has begun to put AIDS in sane perspective. "We can't go on just living through AIDS," the task force's Urvashi Vaid has said. "We have to think in terms of living beyond it if this movement's going to survive." The organization has contained its AIDS expenditures at 15 percent of its total program budget and reinforced its primary work of gay liberation. Yet the task force has a staff of only ten, and some 400 occasional volunteers nationally. New York's G.M.H.C. has a staff of 105, plus 1,900 volunteers. The task force's 1988 budget was a humiliating $860,000—more than $10 million less than the budget of the G.M.H.C. This grotesque disparity is compounded over and over across the nation.

Even otherwise deeply closeted gay men and Lesbians are avid in their testimonials about the need to wage war against the disease. But too many of these AIDS crusaders never go public over the right of homosexuals to something more than not dying. In my gym, a crossroads of Manhattan, a coterie of cultish gay men plastered ACT UP's "Silence = Death" logo everywhere in the facility and are given to working out in ACT UP or G.M.H.C. T-shirts—as though sporting such gym wear were a courageous act. But I've not seen one of that crowd so boldly advertise a more identifiably gay and therefore riskier issue. A certain interest in AIDS has become the trendy code for suggesting one's homosexuality without declaring it, what being a bachelor and an artiste used to suggest.

It isn't a virus that for centuries has deprived us gay men and Lesbians of our freedom.

The ruse that comforts us is that the fight against AIDS and the struggle for gay rights are the same. In 1988, a gay Chicago newspaper headline read "Riverside [California] Supports Gay Rights." The story below read: "The Riverside City Council unanimously approved an ordinance that bans discrimination against people with AIDS." It's in this very sort of thing that we're deceived. What good do those laws do for most Lesbians, who certainly are not suffering from AIDS? Or for the average homosexual or bisexual man, who, whatever our hysteria, would not test positive for HIV either? Or for those who have been exposed to the virus but are asymptomatic, not all of whom will sicken and die, however fantastic the latest rumors? What's the benefit of such legislation to gay men with AIDS themselves if the excuse to abuse their rights isn't AIDS but homosexuality? Any benefit that gay men and Lesbians get from the legislated rights of people with AIDS is second-handed grace: You have to claim to be dying to receive it.

But our failure is far more iniquitous than mere dereliction. For, though the constituencies of gay rights and AIDS activism may overlap, the politics—as conceived—are often violently incompatible. At the October 1987 National March on Washington for Lesbian and Gay Rights, an uncommon show of militant self-respect among homosexuals, at least a half-million of us paraded not just against AIDS but for all the rights and privileges that heterosexuals enjoy. Yet, even as we rallied, I sat in a meeting of national AIDS activists who fretted over the possibility that the event would become a political embarrassment for AIDS lobbyists. The symbolic public same-sex wedding the Saturday before the march, a demonstration for spousal rights, was a particular sore point. The director of a powerful national AIDS umbrella organization especially complained that when the wedding hit the news a disgusted Congress would renege on AIDS funding. She and her colleagues still hoped desperately that last-minute maneuvers would kill the thing—treachery bartering away gay liberation.

AIDS Is Not the Worst Enemy

Some angry lesbians question whether bourgeois gay men ever wanted more than comfortably closeted sex anyway and now wonder if they want more than a quick cure for AIDS in order to get back to the old days. Some ask more bitterly yet whether men, who demand center stage for AIDS, would sacrifice a pittance of their politics or pleasures if Lesbians were the ones dying. Yet, there always have been gay men who've wanted more than sex and obsequious privacy, whose cause has been politically radical and impolite. They've been largely shouted down by the politics of this epidemic. And the more the AIDS movement divorces itself from the demands of gay rights, the more it becomes a route to respect for homosexuals not open to unapologetic gay activists. AIDS is the cause celebre, and, insidiously, we are drawn in, chumming with the Liz Taylors and even the William F. Buckley Jrs. (who've contributed charitably to the fight against AIDS, though Bill has called for tattooing infected gay men's asses). Gossip columnists bold-face AIDS activists' names among mentions of the socially registered. New York's artsy Bessie Committee even gave ACT UP a performance citation last year for its street protests, unlikely applause for genuine revolutionaries.

But even homophobes who'd never want to see a homosexual holding a lover's hand, especially in front of the children, can cry (and contribute) at the thought of so many gay men dying. They're with us on AIDS: Dying and preoccupied with dying, we're less of a threat, our radical potential diverted to mere survival. Through a marriage with disease we've arrived. But to live with our apostasy we've also had to hide from the damning truth that our patrons in the fight against AIDS are seldom dear friends when we're not being sick, just homosexual.

It isn't a virus that for centuries has deprived us gay men and Lesbians of our freedom, nor is it this epidemic that now most destroys our lives. Nor is it bigotry. It's our own shame, a morbid failure of self-respect and sane, selfrighteous anger. If we care about nothing but AIDS now, it is because identifying with sexually transmitted death plays to some dark belief that we deserve it.

In the midst of death, we are confronted with a choice of life that so far we've only dallied with, the terrible responsibility of living free. For wholeness demands more than arguing with bigots, more than crying for acceptance, more than fighting against disease. It asks that we abandon selfishness, self-pity and every compromise of our self-worth. It insists that we nurture the dying, more selflessly than we ever have, but care as much for the promise of life. It compels us to understand that silence equals death not only in the middle of an epidemic, but that it always has killed us and will continue its genocide when AIDS is gone. And wholeness forces us to forsake AIDS as our dark obsession, as the sum of our lives. For this disease is at least as fatal to our hearts as to our blood. Our devotion to it will kill us more surely than a virus ever could.

Timeline: The First Decade of the AIDS Epidemic

1980
Doctors begin to notice unusual ailments, especially *Pneumocystis carinii* pneumonia and Kaposi's sarcoma, and associated immune deficiency among young homosexual men.

May 1981
The *New York Times* publishes a short article about the illnesses, the first mention in the popular press of the condition that would become known as AIDS.

June 5, 1981
The first medical description of the condition appears in the CDC's *Morbidity and Mortality Weekly Report.*

October 1981
The CDC declares the disease an epidemic.

Late 1981
The Gay Men's Health Crisis, the first support group for people with AIDS, is founded.

April 1982
The first congressional hearing on the new disease is held.

May 1982
Robert Gallo of the NIH begins his search for the cause of the mystery ailment, which he suspects is a virus.

June 1982
A meeting at the New York Department of Health reports cases of the disease in intravenous drug users, hemophiliacs, and Haitians as well as homosexuals.

July 1982
Scientists agree to call the new disease AIDS (acquired immune deficiency syndrome).

1983

The CDC warns blood banks that the blood supply may be contaminated with an unknown disease agent.

January 1983

The first cases of heterosexually transmitted AIDS are reported.

May 1983

Luc Montagnier and his colleagues at the Pasteur Institute in France report the isolation of a virus that they call LAV from the cells of AIDS patients.

Summer 1983

Montagnier sends samples of LAV to Robert Gallo.

October 1983

Project SIDA, a multidisciplinary study of AIDS in Zaire, Africa, begins.

April 23, 1984

Margaret Heckler, secretary of the Department of Health and Human Services, holds a press conference to announce that Gallo's laboratory has isolated the virus that appears to cause AIDS, which he calls HTLV-3, and that a test to identify the virus in blood has been developed.

June 1984

Gallo and Montagnier admit that the viruses isolated by their laboratories appear to be identical.

1985

The Pasteur Institute files a lawsuit for a share in the royalties from a blood test for AIDS that both the institute and NIH have attempted to patent; the institute claims that the virus isolated by Gallo came from the French laboratory.

March 1985

The FDA approves the blood test for antibodies to the AIDS virus, and blood banks begin screening their supplies.

April 15–17, 1985

The First International AIDS Conference is held in Atlanta, Georgia.

September 1985
Ryan White, a thirteen-year-old hemophiliac in Indiana who acquired AIDS through blood transfusions, is barred from attending public school classes.

October 2, 1985
Actor Rock Hudson dies of AIDS; his death brings the disease to widespread public attention.

1986
Ryan White successfully sues his school district, obtaining the right to return to school.

May 1986
The virus discovered by Montagnier and Gallo is renamed HIV (human immunodeficiency virus).

September 1986
A large trial of the drug AZT as a treatment for AIDS is stopped because the drug appears to be too effective to withhold from patients.

1987
Larry Kramer founds ACT UP (AIDS Coalition to Unleash Power), a militant AIDS activist organization. Peter Duesberg begins to challenge the claim that HIV causes AIDS. President Ronald Reagan and French Premier Jacques Chirac sign an agreement dividing the royalties for the AIDS blood test between the two countries and the credit for HIV's discovery between the Gallo and Montagnier laboratories. The World Health Organization launches a global program to combat AIDS. Congress passes a law barring HIV-positive noncitizens from entering the United States. ACT UP holds a mass demonstration in New York; shortly afterward, the FDA announces that the approval process for new anti-AIDS drugs will be shortened by two years.

March 1987
President Reagan mentions AIDS publicly for the first time.

March 19, 1987
The FDA approves AZT as the first specific treatment for AIDS.

October 1987
Cleve Jones makes the first panel of the AIDS Memorial Quilt in San Francisco.

1988

The NIH establishes the Office of AIDS Research. The U.S. government mails out 107 million copies of "Understanding AIDS," a booklet by Surgeon General C. Everett Koop.

1989

After intense protests by ACT UP and others, Burroughs Wellcome, the manufacturer of AZT, lowers the drug's price by 20 percent.

1990

Ronald Reagan publicly apologizes for having ignored the AIDS epidemic while he was president.

April 1990

Ryan White dies at age eighteen.

May 1990

President Bush signs the Ryan White Comprehensive AIDS Resource Emergency Act to provide emergency relief to sixteen cities hit hardest by the epidemic; however, Congress appropriates little money to fund the act.

1991

Further tests determine that the virus isolated by Robert Gallo's laboratory came from the Pasteur Institute.

Glossary

ACT UP: AIDS Coalition to Unleash Power, a militant AIDS activist organization formed by playwright and novelist Larry Kramer in 1987.

AIDS: Acquired immune deficiency syndrome, the name agreed on in 1982 for the immune system disorder usually believed to be caused by the human immunodeficiency virus (HIV).

AIDS-related complex (ARC): A collection of symptoms, chiefly enlargement of the lymph glands, that can develop in HIV-positive people and often presages the development of AIDS.

anemia: A deficiency of red blood cells.

antibody: A chemical produced by the immune system that attaches to a particular kind of invader, such as a bacterium or virus; the presence of antibodies to a particular microorganism in a person's blood means that the person has been exposed to that microorganism.

asymptomatic: Without symptoms or signs of a particular illness.

AZT (azidothymidine): The first drug approved by the U.S. Food and Drug Administration (in 1987) for treatment of AIDS; also called zidovudine or Retrovir.

bathhouse: An establishment used as a meeting place for promiscuous sexual encounters by some members of the gay community.

B cell: A type of cell in the immune system that makes antibodies.

biopsy: A medical procedure in which a small sample of tissue is taken from the body for testing.

Castro Street: A street in San Francisco on or near which many gay men lived, beginning in the 1970s; the name was sometimes used to represent the San Francisco gay community as a whole.

CD4 T cell: The type of immune system cell that HIV infects and destroys; sometimes called a helper T cell or T4 lymphocyte.

Centers for Disease Control and Prevention (CDC): An organization in Atlanta, Georgia, sponsored by the U.S. government and dedicated to preventing, tracking, and controlling disease, injury, and disability.

chemotherapy: Drug treatment for illness, especially the use of fairly toxic drugs to treat cancer.

ELISA test: Enzyme-linked immunosorbent assay, a test that identifies blood infected with HIV by recognizing antibodies to the virus.

enteric: Related to the intestine or gut.

epidemiologist: A scientist who studies the way disease spreads in populations.

hemophiliac: A person, almost always a male, who suffers from an inherited disease that prevents the blood from clotting; hemophiliacs must have frequent transfusions of blood or blood products. Many hemophiliacs contracted AIDS in the late 1970s or early 1980s from blood contaminated with HIV.

hepatitis B: A serious liver disease caused by a virus that, like HIV, is spread through sexual contact and blood.

HIV: Human immunodeficiency virus, the name agreed on in 1986 for the retrovirus usually believed to cause AIDS.

HIV positive: Showing antibodies to HIV or other evidence of having been infected by the virus; people who are HIV positive may or may not show any signs of illness.

HTLV-1: A retrovirus identified by Robert Gallo in the 1970s as the cause of a type of human leukemia; he later found a second cancer-causing retrovirus, HTLV-2.

HTLV-3: The name that Robert Gallo gave to the virus later called HIV.

immune system: The body's defense system against microorganisms and other disease-causing invaders, consisting of cells and chemicals in the blood and another circulating body fluid, lymph.

immunologist: A scientist who studies the immune system.

infectious disease: A disease caused by a microorganism.

intravenous drug use: Use of drugs that must be injected into a vein, such as heroin.

in vitro: In a laboratory test tube or dish, as opposed to a living body (literally, "in glass").

Kaposi's sarcoma: A cancerlike illness, marked by purple spots on the skin, that affects some people with AIDS; it has proved to be caused by a herpesvirus (a different kind of virus from HIV).

latent period: A period after infection by a microorganism during which no signs of disease appear; the latent period for HIV infection can be ten years or more.

LAV: The name given by Luc Montagnier and his colleagues at the Pasteur Institute in France to the virus they isolated from AIDS patients, later called HIV.

leukemia: A cancer in which excessive numbers of white blood cells (immune system cells) are produced.

lymphadenopathy: The medical condition of having swollen or diseased lymph nodes.

lymph nodes (lymph glands): Lumps of tissue found in various parts of the body, such as under the arms, that make certain kinds of immune system cells and filter out and destroy invading microorganisms; swollen lymph glands can be a sign of infection by a microorganism.

lymphocyte: An immune system cell, such as a B cell or a T cell.

mutation: A change in a gene or genes.

National Institutes of Health (NIH): A group of large medical research institutions in Bethesda, Maryland, sponsored by the U.S. government.

palliative care: Health care given to increase a patient's comfort rather than to cure disease; often given to people for whom no cure is possible.

placebo: An inactive substance or treatment, usually given (without a patient's knowledge) for comparison purposes during a test of a new drug or medical treatment.

***Pneumocystis carinii*:** A microscopic parasite that can cause pneumonia (a serious lung disease) in people with poorly functioning immune systems, such as people with AIDS.

poppers: Inhaled stimulant drugs, usually amyl or butyl nitrites, reputed to have an aphrodisiac effect and used by some male homosexuals; some scientists believed that they played a role in causing AIDS.

protocol: A set of rules and procedures to be followed during a medical test or course of treatment.

PWA: A person with AIDS.

resistance: The ability that organisms develop, usually through genetic mutation, to fight off or survive chemicals that formerly killed that type of organism.

retrovirus: One of a group of viruses that has genetic material made of RNA rather than DNA and possesses an enzyme, reverse transcriptase, that allows the virus's genetic material to be copied into the genome (collection of genes) of the cells it infects; HIV is a retrovirus.

reverse transcriptase: An enzyme possessed by retroviruses that allows them to copy their genetic material into the genome (collection of genes) of the cells they infect so that their genes are reproduced along with the cell's each time the cell divides.

RNA: Ribonucleic acid, a chemical that carries genetic information in certain viruses and plays a part in the expression of genetic information in other organisms.

syndrome: A group of symptoms (signs of illness) that usually occur together and often have a single cause.

T cell: A type of cell in the immune system; HIV attacks one form of T cell.

T4 lymphocyte: Another name for the CD4 T cell, the kind of immune system cell that HIV attacks.

virulent: Greatly infectious and capable of causing serious disease.

zidovudine: Another name for AZT (azidothymidine), the first drug approved in the United States for the treatment of AIDS.

For Further Research

Books

Ronald Bayer and Gerald M. Oppenheimer, *AIDS Doctors: Voices from the Epidemic, an Oral History*. New York: Oxford University Press, 2000.

Virginia Berridge and Philip Strong, eds., *AIDS and Contemporary History*. England: Cambridge University Press, 1993.

Steve Connor and Sharon Kingman, *The Search for the Virus: The Scientific Discovery of AIDS and the Quest for a Cure*. New York: Penguin Books, 1988.

John Crewdson, *Science Fictions: A Scientific Mystery, a Massive Cover-Up, and the Dark Legacy of Robert Gallo*. Boston: Little, Brown, 2002.

Douglas Crimp, ed., *AIDS: Cultural Analysis, Cultural Activism*. Cambridge, MA: MIT Press, 1988.

Michael Anthony DiSpezio, *The Science, Spread, and Therapy of HIV Disease: Everything You Need to Know but Had No Idea Who to Ask*. Shrewsbury, MA: ATL Press, 1998.

Peter H. Duesberg, *Inventing the AIDS Virus*. Washington, DC: Regnery, 1997.

Hung Fan et al., *AIDS: Science and Society*. Boston: Jones & Bartlett, 1997.

Douglas A. Feldman and Julia Wang Miller, *The AIDS Crisis: A Documentary History*. Westport, CT: Greenwood Press, 1998.

Michael Fumento, *The Myth of Heterosexual AIDS*. Washington, DC: Regnery, 1993.

Robert C. Gallo, *Virus Hunting: AIDS, Cancer, and the Human Retrovirus: A Story of Scientific Discovery*. New York: HarperCollins, 1991.

Christine Grady, *The Search for an AIDS Vaccine: Ethical Issues in the Development and Testing of a Preventive HIV Vaccine*. Bloomington: Indiana University Press, 1995.

Mirko Drazen Grmek, ed., *History of AIDS: Emergence and Origin of a Modern Pandemic*. NJ: Princeton University Press, 1993.

Caroline Hannaway, Victoria A. Harden, and John Parascandola, eds., *AIDS and the Public Debate: Historical and Contemporary Perspectives*. Washington, DC: IOS Press, 1995.

Robert Klitzman, *Being Positive: The Lives of Men and Women with HIV.* Chicago: Ivan R. Dee, 1997.

Larry Kramer and Simon Watney, *Reports from the Holocaust: The Story of an AIDS Activist*. New York: St. Martin's Press, 1994.

Christine Maggiore, *What If Everything You Thought You Knew About AIDS Was Wrong?* Studio City, CA: American Foundation for AIDS Alternatives, 2000.

Luc Montagnier, *Virus*. New York: W.W. Norton, 2000.

William B. Rubenstein et al., *The Rights of People Who Are HIV Positive: The Authoritative ACLU Guide to the Rights of People Living with HIV Disease and AIDS*. Carbondale: Southern Illinois University Press, 1996.

Kate Scannell, *Death of the Good Doctor: Lessons from the Heart of the AIDS Epidemic*. San Francisco: Cleis Press, 1999.

Barry D. Schoub, *AIDS and HIV in Perspective: A Guide to Understanding the Virus and Its Consequences*. New York: Cambridge University Press, 1999.

Benjamin Heim Shepard, *White Nights and Ascending Shadows: An Oral History of the San Francisco AIDS Epidemic*. Herndon, VA: Cassell, 1997.

Randy Shilts, *And the Band Played On: Politics, People, and the AIDS Epidemic*. New York: St. Martin's Press, 1987.

Alvin Silverstein, Virginia B. Silverstein, and Laura Silverstein Nunn, *AIDS: An All-About Guide for Young Adults*. Berkeley Heights, NJ: Enslow, 1999.

Raymond A. Smith, ed., *The Encyclopedia of AIDS: A Social, Political, Cultural, and Scientific Record of the HIV Epidemic*. Chicago: Fitzroy Dearborn, 1998.

Patricia Thomas, *Big Shot: Passion, Politics, and the Struggle for an AIDS Vaccine*. New York: PublicAffairs, 2001.

Periodicals

AIDS Weekly, "Twenty Years of AIDS Ravages Societies, Young and Old, Around the World," December 17, 2001.

W. Blattner, Robert C. Gallo, and H.M. Temin, "HIV Causes AIDS," *Science*, July 29, 1988.

Mark Bregman, "AIDS at 20: Will We Find a Cure?" *Science World*, October 1, 2001.

Joseph Carey, "An AIDS Pill That Offers Hope," *U.S. News & World Report*, September 29, 1986.

Centers for Disease Control and Prevention, "HIV and AIDS: United States, 1981–2000," *Journal of the American Medical Association*, June 27, 2001.

Jon Cohen, "The Duesberg Phenomenon," *Science*, December 9, 1994.

Geoffrey Cowley, "A Tempest in a Test Tube," *Newsweek*, March 18, 1991.

Sara Davidson, "'I'm Going to Fight This,'" *People Weekly*, June 16, 1986.

Robert C. Gallo, "My Life Stalking AIDS," *Discover*, October 1989.

David Gelman, "The Social Fallout from an Epidemic," *Newsweek*, August 12, 1985.

Ken Gross, "Larry Kramer: Refusing to Go Quietly: An Angry Playwright Calls Down the Furies Against Indifference to AIDS," *People Weekly*, July 9, 1990.

Gina Kolata, "Congress, NIH Open Coffers for AIDS," *Science*, July 29, 1983.

Charles Krauthammer, "The Politics of a Plague: Illness as Metaphor Revisited," *New Republic*, August 1, 1983.

John Leo, "The Real Epidemic: Fear and Despair," *Time*, July 4, 1983.

J. Allen McCutchan, "What You Can Do to Stop the AIDS Panic," *RN*, October 1986.

Colin Norman, "AIDS Priority Fight Goes to Court," *Science*, January 3, 1986.

Judith Randal, "Too Little Aid for AIDS," *Technology Review*, August/September 1984.

Michael S. Serrill, "Public Health: A Scourge Spreads Panic," *Time*, October 28, 1985.

Myrna E. Watanabe, "AIDS 20 Years Later," *Scientist*, June 11, 2001.

Websites

AIDS Education and Global Information System (AEGIS), "The HIV/AIDS Encyclopedia," 2002. www.aegis.org.

AIDS History Project, University of California, San Francisco, 1999. www.library.ucsf.edu.

AIDS Project Los Angeles, "AIDS Timeline, 2001." www.apla.org.
CNN, "AIDS: 20 Years of an Epidemic," 2001. www.cnn.com.
Kaiser Family Foundation, "AIDS at 20," 2000. www.kff.org.
National Institutes of Health, "In Their Own Words . . . NIH Researchers Recall the Early Years of AIDS," 2000. http://aidshistory.nih.gov.
San Francisco AIDS Oral History Series, "The AIDS Epidemic in San Francisco: The Medical Response, 1981–1984," vols. 1–7. University of California, Berkeley, 1995–1999. http://sunsite.berkeley.edu.

Index